Is Perfect Good Enough?

Ernest Cataldo

Is Perfect Good Enough? by Ernest Cataldo

Independently Published

ISBN: 9781980944126

© 2018 Ernest Cataldo

All rights reserved.
No part of this book may be reproduced in
any form without written permission.

perfect.good.enough@gmail.com

Cover photo taken in East Berlin (1966) by Donna Cataldo

This book is dedicated to Mimi.
There never has been a better mother-in-law.
She was one of us-- young at heart.

"Too late, I found you can't wait to become perfect, you got to go out and fall down and get up with everybody else."

— Ray Bradbury,
Something Wicked This Way Comes

"It's amazing all the different things your average guy might need a lawyer for."

--- David Frishberg,
My Attorney Bernie

Table of Contents

Preface
Honeymoon..1
Growing Up..9
Radio Days..16
The Strangler..24
Falling for Donna..28
MIT..34
Paul...38
Father Knows Best?....................................46
Hey, Baby..53
Uncle Sal...56
SAE...69
Road Trip..74
Selective Service..82
The Shrink..86
The Motorcycle File...................................88
Mrs. Miller..96
Odd Jobs...100
Wild Bill..107
Grandparents..112
Uncle Arnie...116

The Beard	119
Kids	124
The Secret	131
The King and I	133
Baseball Memories	137
Wedding Gifts	144
CSI Beacon Hill	147
Is Perfect Good Enough?	151
My Weddings	156
Meeting Stephen Hawking	159
Bongo	162
Earthquake	166
Car Salesmen	170
The Count Lipsky Affair	174
Real Estate	178
Two Waiters	182
Checkmate	186
Good Byes	190
Remembering Pete and me	195
Afterward	
Acknowledgments	

Preface

I wrote this collection of memories mainly for my grandchildren, so they might get to know their Papa a little better. I know almost nothing of my grandparents and regretfully, I started too late to gather many stories from my Mom and Dad. Now most have been lost.

Over the years, I have been so fortunate to be surrounded by many interesting people and I hope through these stories I have been able to make clear what they brought into my life, as well as the humor of one of my dad's hare-brained schemes or the sense of awe when you see one of your children for the first time or the embarrassment of having to admit to making a world-class, stupid mistake.

I don't pretend to have an impressive memory but I've tried to be faithful to the spirit of the moments described. I've changed a few names to avoid hurt feelings, unnecessary embarrassment and law suits, but everything written here is how I remember it.

Just as world history is written by the victors, I suppose you could say that personal history is written by those who bother to write it... and I'm writing it.

As Huckleberry Finn said of his author, "*That book was made by Mr. Mark Twain, and he told the truth, mainly. There was things which he stretched, but mainly he told the truth.*"

Anyway, this is my side of the story... and I'm standing by it.

E. Cataldo
Boston
2018

l-r: sister Sue, cousin Dotty, neighbor Ann, me, cousin Mary, cousin Lucy, and neighbor Carol (1949)

Honeymoon

Donna and I had to get married... and before June 15th. You see, that was the day the MIT British Eagle charter flight to London departed New York's JFK airport and our honeymoon started. So the date of the wedding was set for Sunday, June 12, 1966... and that was only eleven days away.

My memory of the events leading up to the marriage ceremony is somewhat clouded by fifty-odd years of story telling, wishful thinking and misinterpretation of my youthful arrogance but I won't let that stop me from trying to recall them.

Donna and I had been dating since just before I entered college in September, 1962. Then, after I pledged Sigma Alpha Epsilon (and even before I was initiated), she was a fixture at the fraternity house on Beacon Street. Very few weekends went by that we weren't together; and summers... we were inseparable. Whatever image the phrase *young people in love* conjures up in your mind; that was us. Not that I gave it (or anything else for that matter) a lot of thought back then, but in my simple mind's view it seemed we might just stay together always.

Then, before Christmas, 1965, Donna said to me, "We need to talk."

She told me she thought we should, perhaps, not settle down so fast, get to be with other people and see how we felt after a while. This was a bit of a shock to me because I thought we were already settled down, I

Donna and me (1963)

didn't want to see other people and I already knew how I felt. But of course she had been very young when we met and...

Looking back, I'd say a good one word description of me then was... heartbroken. I moped about the fraternity house, missed classes and found myself walking around Boston and Cambridge when (maybe) I should have been studying. Without much focus, I applied to and was accepted into USC engineering graduate school and likewise applied to the government Teacher Corps, where I was tentatively assigned to Athens, Ohio in the Fall. But I didn't *really* know what I wanted to do. The future seemed very, very uncertain.

Then around that time, I heard one of my fraternity brothers talk about his adventures motorcycling around Europe alone the previous summer and it sounded so wonderful that I decided right then, *"That's what I should do."* The fact that I'd never even been *on* a motorcycle before didn't seem at all important.

How hard could it be? I thought.

I bought a ticket on an MIT summer charter flight to London, got a passport, a smallpox shot, some traveler's checks and a five dollar camera. The plane would leave on June 15th from New York. I had something to look forward to; I just had to manage until then.

One Friday night in March, during a fraternity house party, my roommate Jeff brought a date up to our room. When they entered, I instinctively started to clear out.

"No, please don't leave because of us," she said.

I stopped and looked at her. She was blonde and cute. Then I looked at Jeff and he seemed indifferent. I was feeling lonely, so that was enough for me. I stayed and we talked for a while.

Her name was Elizabeth. I asked about her accent and learned that her family moved to New York from South Africa when she was eight and now she was a sophomore at Wellesley College. She liked America once she learned everyone here wasn't a member of the Jets or the Sharks. (Just before leaving Johannesburg she had seen *West Side Story*.)

After they left, I practiced the guitar until about midnight then had just gotten into bed when a pledge appeared and told me I had a phone call from 'some girl.' It was Elizabeth and (long-story-short) we ended up out on a date the next night. She was easy to be with, a good listener and nice enough, but she did have one big problem... she wasn't Donna. Still, by the end of May, Elizabeth and I were going out pretty steadily, so I told her all about my upcoming trip.

She said, "I wish I could come along," and I told her I'd be back early in September and the time would fly by, etc... etc. We made a date for the following week, so that we could see each other before I left on my trip and before she went back home to Long Island for the summer.

When I mentioned to my mom that I was dating a girl from South Africa, she told me not to worry; it was okay with her.

"My best friend in high school was black," she said.

Typical of my mother, even when she didn't quite *get it,* she still offered me encouragement.

So I had survived the spring but it was pretty clear as the term neared an end that my screwing off meant that I wasn't going to have enough credits to graduate in June. Fortunately, I hadn't lost interest in my undergraduate thesis, so to salvage some credits, I finished it. Now I simply had to get it typed and hand it in. In my previous life, Donna (who had attended Chandler school, where she learned shorthand and typing) would have typed it for me. In fact, before the breakup, she had said she would.

Here, things get a little unclear. One of two things happened next.

Either--

I called Donna and reminded her that she had promised to type my thesis, in hopes of seeing her again. If I did, I'm a genius and it was the smartest thing I (or any other human being) ever did. And that's why... I don't think I did.

Or--

Donna called *me* to remind me that she had promised to type my thesis, in hopes of seeing me again. If that's what happened, then I was just the knucklehead I recall being, and she was a genius.

It doesn't really matter which version is correct, it was a win-win. In any case, a call was made, offer accepted and at the end of May, 1966, Donna arrived at the fraternity house to type my thesis.

The typing went well enough, then at one point we took a break and because the term had just ended, the house was pretty quiet. Mrs. Miller, the cook, and Joseph, the butler were off until fall, so Joseph's room, with it's small twin bed where he napped between meals, was empty. On our way to the kitchen to see what might be around for a snack, we passed by Joseph's room.

"Look," I said, stopping at the open door, "That's the picture of Joseph and his regiment from World War I."

We walked in the room and I could feel the energy building, blood rushing to my head, the room whirling. We kissed. A *we haven't kissed in six months* kiss. I closed the door... there was no stopping.

The next day or two are just a blur but I know we walked and talked about what we had been doing and who we had been with and what we should do next. I told her about my motorcycle trip to Europe, coming up in just two weeks. We had some serious choices to make.

While walking through the Boston Public Garden, I chose to ask her to marry me and she chose to say, "yes."

"And why wait? Let's get married right away and... we can go to Europe together," I said, "It'll be our honeymoon."

"But we can't elope," Donna said, "Our parents would die. And it should be in a church... I don't want to hurt them."

"No problem. We'll have a small wedding. Just close --"

Donna interrupted, "We could get married at the MIT chapel, then a reception with just friends and family at my house or your Dad's patio."

"Perfect," I said, "Let's go tell them."

We announced our intention and it must have been pretty clear that they had no choice in the matter so after a few seconds they congratulated us. There were only eleven days until the wedding and I remember they said not to worry; they would arrange everything. We gave them a list of twenty or so friends we wanted to be there and left the details to them.

"Just tell us where to be on the twelfth," we said, "and we'll be there."

To fulfill a requirement for a Catholic wedding I went to see our local parish priest and in one of the most bizarre conversations I've ever been a party to; he told me:

1. That we couldn't have the wedding at the MIT chapel because other religions used it.

2. In order to have a wedding at the parish church, the 'banns' had to be read for three consecutive Sundays and there was

absolutely no way around it. Three weeks minimum.

3. That God intended sex solely for procreation-- not pleasure-- so "don't overdo it."

4. And if I found things weren't going well in my married life, I should "remember to try flowers."

Donna and I reluctantly agreed to forget the MIT chapel and have the wedding at the local church but there was no way we could wait three weeks, so the fathers swung into action and bribed the parish priest to agree to a compromise. He would indeed, read the banns three times as required... but for a five hundred dollar cash donation he would read them *all* on the upcoming Sunday.

Donna and I both had the required blood tests then went to town hall to get a marriage license.

"While we're here," Donna said as we climbed the steps, "Let's get a dog license for Snoopy."

Snoopy, the best dog who ever lived, was a wire haired fox terrier I had given Donna on our first Christmas together and who would be living with us after the honeymoon.

So in the town clerk's office we filled out the paperwork for both licenses and slid it across the counter to the clerk.

"You haven't finished filling this one out," she said, "You left *color of applicants* blank."

"Which license is that?" I asked mockingly.

"This isn't a joke," she replied, "You have to fill in your color."

"That's crazy," I said, "this is 1966. I'm not filling in my color."

Donna nodded in agreement.

"Well then, I'll write it in for you," the clerk said.

"Why on Earth does the town need to know our color?" we both asked.

"It's not for the town, it's for you. So you can be sure what color your partner really is."

Donna and I giggled.

I held up my bare arm, Donna studied it and said, "Hmm, I'd say off-white... peach maybe."

The clerk wasn't amused.

When she finished writing in our color, she put the marriage license application on her desk and slid the dog license toward me.

I said, "Is that it? Do we have to do anything else?"

Now, the clerk thought I was talking about the dog license, so she replied, "No."

Never having been married before, I didn't realize there was a waiting period and I was supposed to go back to pick up the marriage license in three days.

We still had so many things to do. For one, we had to get Donna a plane ticket. I called Nick, my fraternity brother who ran Tech Travel (an MIT student run travel agency at the time.)

"Nick, I need another ticket for the charter to London."

"Are you kidding? It's been sold out for a month," he replied, "Why?"

"Donna and I are getting married next week and she's coming with me, that's why."

"Married?" he said, "I thought--," then after a few seconds of silence, "I'll call you back."

That evening he called and reported, "All set. She has a seat."

"That's great Nick, but how--"

"Well, let's just say someone may be a little upset on the fifteenth. Just enjoy your honeymoon."

"Will do," I said, "Thanks."

The next day Donna went to the Federal Building and got a passport (issued in her maiden name.)

Oh... and remember that date I had made with Elizabeth last week? Well, what I should have done was cancel it --or-- go on the date and tell her I was getting married --or-- just commit suicide. Anything, except what I did do, which was see her and say goodbye and let her assume we would see each other again in September... an idiotic mistake that I would soon regret.

We had a rehearsal at the church the night before the wedding. You walk here, not too fast, hold this, go there, etc. At some point the priest asked me where the marriage license was.

"I don't know. I thought you would have it," I said.

"Oh, dear," he said.

Oh dear, indeed, I thought.

The wedding was tomorrow!

After a frantic few minutes, Mimi (Donna's wonderful mother) said, "My friend Marie works at town hall. I'll call her."

The call was made; Marie had a key to town hall, knew the

combination to the clerk's safe, retrieved the license and literally saved the day.

```
                NOTICE—Alterations and Erasures in this Certificate are forbidden.       No. 90

                         Commonwealth of Massachusetts
                                Town of Winthrop

                         Certificate of Marriage
                  (If this Certificate is not used within sixty days it must be returned to the Town Clerk)
                GROOM                                           BRIDE
FULL NAME                                  FULL NAME   Also maiden name. If widowed or divorced
         ERNEST ALFRED CATALDO                              DONNA LALLI MABUKELLI
AGE AT LAST                                AGE AT LAST
BIRTHDAY    21  (Years)     COLOR          BIRTHDAY   18  (Years)    COLOR
                            White                                    White
RESIDENCE                                  RESIDENCE
         55 Banks Street, Winthrop                   205 Somerset Avenue, Winthrop
NUMBER OF           WIDOWED                NUMBER OF             WIDOWED
MARRIAGE   First    OR DIVORCED   --       MARRIAGE   First      OR DIVORCED   --
OCCUPATION                                 OCCUPATION
           Student                                    At Home
BIRTHPLACE                                 BIRTHPLACE
         Winthrop, Massachusetts                      Winthrop, Massachusetts
```

Our proof of color.

    June 12th was warm and sunny. My brother-in-law Bill was my best man and Donna was the prettiest girl I had ever seen in her white sun-dress and veil. The parents had arranged everything in eleven days! A limousine picked us up at the church and whisked us off to Polcari's Italian Restaurant in the North End, where 400 guests awaited! The fathers had gone to a lot of weddings and this was payback time.

    That evening we flew with a bag of checks and cash to New York City, where we had to argue with the hotel staff to avoid a room with four twin beds on our wedding night! The next day we opened a bank account, bought some traveler's checks and saw some sights. Three days later we took a bus to JFK airport and checked in for our flight. While we were sitting in the waiting area I noticed someone all too familiar walking toward us.

    "Donna," I said with urgency, "Do me a favor and go to the ladies room."

    "What? Why would--"

    "Please! I'll explain later. Just go!"

    Bewildered, she walked off toward the ladies room.

    Elizabeth had come to see me off.

    "Hi Elizabeth," I said, "I have something to tell you. Do you see that woman there; the one entering the ladies room?"

    It was without a doubt, the most incredibly awkward moment of my entire life. Elizabeth walked away and never looked back. I realized what an idiot I had been, but there was nothing I could do about it.

"Shit. Shit. Shit!" I muttered.

I felt as if I had shrunk to two feet tall. Donna returned and I explained that I had thought it would be easier and less hurtful to not mention my upcoming marriage on that last date with Elizabeth. I figured, I'd be away... she'd forget about me...

I could only guess that Donna might be thinking, *Really? And how did that work out?*

But instead, she gave me a hug. We were in this together. We were man and wife.

Then they called the flight and our honeymoon began.

Growing Up

I'm standing in my backyard holding my mother's hand and watching our house on Main Street burn down. That's my very first memory. It didn't actually burn down completely, but the back portion was so badly damaged we had to move out for a while until it was rebuilt. The fire marshal determined that someone had started the fire in an attached shed and the next morning two uniformed firemen met Mom and me at the site of the fire, where they asked if they could talk with me... *alone*.

I remember seeing the blackened skeleton that had been the rear of my home and being made to sit on the surviving concrete steps between the two firemen. Their uniforms were the kind that they wore in parades... not for fighting fires. There was a strong smell of smoke in the air and after a minute, one of them began to speak as if I wasn't there.

"Hey Bill," he said, looking past me, "I really like to play with matches. How about you?"

The fireman sitting on my other side replied, "Oh, ya Fred, I like it too. It sure is fun."

Now they both looked down at me and one asked, "I'll bet *you* like to play with matches too, don't you, little guy?"

Granted, I was only four years old, but I could sense something wasn't quite right. *Of course* I liked to play with matches... but every adult I had ever met had warned me not to, especially my mother.

So why were these grownups acting like it's okay? I thought.

After a few seconds I said, "No, I'm not allowed to."

Silence followed as they reconsidered their strategy, then I blurted out, "but Victor Dominic plays with them all the time."

"And where does *he* live," they both asked in unison.

I pointed to a house two doors down. They thanked my mother and were quickly gone.

I don't know what the result of the subsequent investigation was, but Victor apparently beat the rap because a year or so later he was in Miss Underhill's first grade class with me, where he became a sort of Center Elementary School legend. He disrupted every class, ate the paste glue, drank the ink and looked under all the girls' skirts. He was always trying to steal my answers in class and after school he made fun of me when I wouldn't smoke a cigarette with him behind his garage. Fortunately, I didn't have much contact with Victor after he was kept back in the first grade. I wouldn't be surprised if he was still there (or probably more likely in jail.)

By the way, I had an alibi for the fire. I was in the kitchen with my mother when my aunt Bea banged on the door telling us, "Run for your lives, the house is on fire!"

All three of us ran down the front stairs and out on to Main Street to safety.

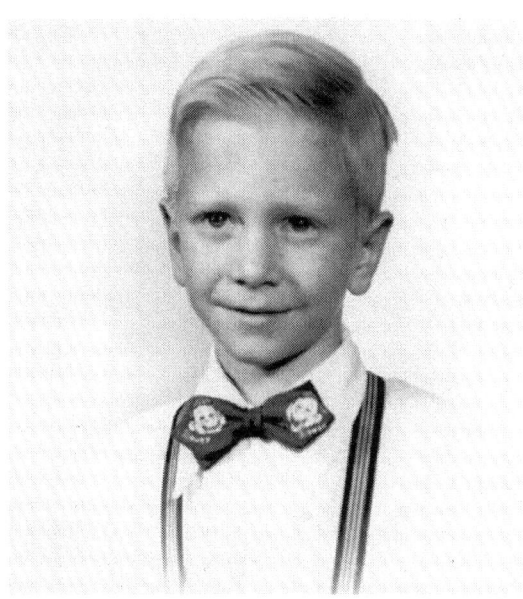

1st Grade with Howdy Doody tie(1950)

. . .

By 1948, the war had been over for three years and my parent's lives had mostly returned to normal. My dad had switched from working at the Watertown Arsenal, where he had machined parts for M1 rifles, to the Coast Guard as a mechanic maintaining lighthouses. The *Office of Price Administration* finally deregulated new kitchen appliances and they were becoming available again, but we still had the wooden ice box that had been in our kitchen since the old fridge broke before I was born. It was literally an oak chest with a door on the side. It had ice in the bottom and food stored above and my only household chore was to empty the water that melted into the metal drain pan on the floor (for which I received an ice cream cone a week at Walsh's Drugstore.) Every few days the ice-man would stop his horse-drawn wagon in front of the house, chop what I now know was a sixty pound chunk (one cubic foot) from a huge block of ice and gripping it with tongs, throw it over his shoulder and muscle it up a flight of stairs to our kitchen.

After being paid, he invariably would rub my hair and say, "Be sure to go to school kid, so you don't end up doing this."

I knew he must be joking of course, as I couldn't imagine anything I'd rather do when I grew up. As the ice melted, that pan filled and got pretty heavy, so my attempts to empty it into the sink met with varying degrees of success. I usually resorted to carrying cups-full over to the sink. A good deal of the liquid ended up on the floor.

"It's only water," my mother would say to make me feel better as we mopped up the kitchen.

Then one day, there was a knock on the door. It was the future. Two men came in and carried the oak and brass ice box away, replacing it a few minutes later with a tall, shiny white metal box with a large cylinder on top. It stood on four legs and resembled a robot I'd seen on a Popular Science magazine cover at the drugstore.

"What's that?" I inquired.

A burly man with an anchor tattooed on his arm answered, "It's your new ice box,"

"Where's the drain pan?" I asked.

"You see this?" he held up the electric plug, "You plug this in the wall and those coils on top make it cold inside. No ice, so no melting."

"No drain pan?" I said, while thinking, *What about my ice cream cone?*

"Then why is it called an *ice box*?" I asked.

The other man said, "That's a good point."

The tattooed man said, "It's real name is a Norge Electric refrigerator." He pulled opened the door. "Look, it even has a light bulb inside."

"Whoa," I exclaimed, "cool!"

It really did have a light bulb inside and no matter how quickly or often I opened the door, that light came on. I checked it many times during that day but when my dad came home and I showed him, he didn't seem impressed.

"Stop doing that. You'll let all the cold out," he said.

The electric refrigerator eliminated my favorite chore (and I don't think I ever saw the ice-man or his horse again) but it did have a freezer compartment where mom kept ice cream right in the house. Maybe the future wouldn't be so bad.

. . .

When I was nine we were in a terrible car accident. I was sitting in the back seat (over the hump as usual) with my Mom on my left and Grandma on my right. Dad was driving when a car sped through a stop sign and hit the passenger side of our car. Mom's head went through the window next to her and I flew over the front seat and struck my dad's elbow as he threw up his arms to protect himself. There were no seatbelts or safety glass back then. I remember that it got very still for a second then there was steam or smoke everywhere. Grandma, who was blind, began screaming in Italian. Mom was quiet. I had bounced back onto the rear seat, with a big lump on my head and was covered in blood. A single ambulance arrived and they decided that the bloodiest (and youngest) victim should be transferred to the hospital first. So off I went; now thoroughly convinced that I was near death.
Minutes later, I was on a table with bright lights shining down. It wasn't heaven but Winthrop Community Hospital where a doctor and nurses set about cutting off my tee shirt with scissors. I was frightened and recalled my mother always telling me to put on clean underwear, *"in case you get in an accident."*

They cleaned my head and arms with swabs, looking for the lacerations. After a moment, the frantic motion stopped suddenly.

The doctor stepped back, pulled off his rubber gloves, threw them to the floor and said, "There's nothing wrong with this kid. Get him out of here!"

A nurse spoke up, "Who's blood was it then?"

It was my mother's.

She almost died that night, was transported in the second ambulance and was kept in the hospital for weeks. Grandma was fine, as was Dad. Of course he wouldn't have told anyone if he was hurt anyway. The newspaper story the next day said I was *twelve* years old. I thought that was the coolest thing ever.

. . .

Two years later we moved into the new house my dad had built on Banks Street very near to Fort Banks, an active army base. The fort had an eight foot high chain link fence around it, topped with razor wire and it was patrolled by military police in jeeps. Since we played baseball in a vacant lot across the street from the fort and many a home run ended up in there, we became quite proficient at scaling the fence. One of my friends (Bobby Raitman) told us that he heard there was an electric chair on the base in one of the old concrete bunkers that were built as shore defenses during one of the World Wars.

So one day, four or five of us jumped the fence and armed with a flashlight went in search of the electric chair. The first abandoned bunker we came to was clearly showing signs of decay. Weeds were growing through cracks in the concrete and its weathered steel door stood ajar, rusted open. Bobby went in ahead, walking very slowly with the flashlight while the rest of us followed closely. It was dim and damp and much cooler than outside. Bobby went down some stairs and turned a corner. It was pitch-black, we couldn't even see our feet except where Bobby pointed the light beam. He went around another corner, walked some more then stopped and let out a shriek, turned and still carrying the only flashlight, ran back out as fast as he could. It happened too quickly for us to keep up, so we had to feel our way along the walls in the total darkness and hope we were going in the right direction. After a few minutes, a few wrong turns and a lot of yelling, we finally saw daylight. We stepped back out onto the grass and were greeted by two MPs in full military gear. White helmets, night sticks, boots and maybe even guns.

One grabbed me by the collar, lifted me into the jeep and said, "What's your name?"

I was scared to death, so I told him.

"Where do you live?"

I was scared to death, so I told him.

I looked around. It seemed everyone else had escaped.

The other MP got behind the wheel and drove us out of the main gate and over to Banks Street, parked in front of my house and walked me to the front door.

Now, no one, *ever* was allowed to use the front door at my house. Not me, not my friends, not my aunts and uncles; even my sister's boyfriend was supposed to use the side door. So now my Dad would have even more reason to be mad. The MP rang the bell. My dad opened the door half way.

"Sir, is this your son?" The MP asked.

"Yes. What's this about?"

I was a dead man and I knew it.

"He was found trespassing on federal government property, sir," he announced sternly. "What would you like done with him?"

Dad opened the door as wide as it would go. I still half expected him to tell us to go around to the side door.

"I'll take care of him," Dad said, "Leave it to me."

"Yes sir," the MP replied crisply. He then turned, hopped in the jeep and drove off.

I was a dead man and I knew it.

Dad closed the door, stood in front of me and said sternly, "Tell me what happened."

I recounted the afternoon's events including the bunker, the electric chair, the flashlight, the shriek, the darkness and my eventual capture. I couldn't even begin to imagine what my dad would do next.

"Do you think he saw an electric chair?" he asked.

"What?"

"Did he really see one?"

"He might have," I said tentatively. "He was pretty scared."

"I'll bet he was. Did he get caught too?"

"I don't think so. He was first out," I said. "He had the flashlight."

"Hmm," my dad mused, "Why do you suppose there would be an electric chair in there?

I thought for a few seconds then said, "Spies. I suppose... to electrocute spies maybe."

"Maybe..." he said, but he didn't sound at all convinced, "...but do me a favor. Stay on *this* side of the fence and let the Army handle the spies, okay?"

"Okay," I said.

I could hardly believe there was no punishment. And... I got to come in the front door!

The next day Bobby Raitman swore to us, he not only *did* see an electric chair but there was someone strapped in it!

"Jeez, how dumb do you think we are?" we all chided.

"Boy, he's an idiot," we said to each other.

I did go on the other side of the fence a few times after that to retrieve home run balls, but I never quite found the time to go back to the bunker.

Radio Days

Normally I left Saint John's Elementary school on the Ocean View Street side and walked directly home; but not on this day. This day I had a mission. So I convinced Sister Clarita to let me out on the Lincoln Street side and headed to the Winthrop Public library. It was a bright fall day in 1953 and I wasn't even distracted by passing the penny candy shoppe on Herman Street (on any other day I would have stopped and spent five cents on a Powerhouse or Baby Ruth bar) but today I had no time for such things. That morning, *Our Weekly Reader* newspaper had been delivered to my 4th grade classroom and in it was an article about people *going to the Moon* someday. I couldn't think of anything else all day... I had to find out how to get to the Moon.

I had asked Sister Jude, "Sister, where can I find out how to go to the Moon?"

"Now why would you do a thing like that?" she replied, "If the good Lord wanted people to-- "

I stopped paying attention at that point and that's when I decided it was time to use my recently obtained public library card. The library wasn't far; located adjacent to the Town Hall near the center. I climbed the imposing steps of the big stone building, managed to get the sizable wooden door open by myself then entered and stood in front of the desk. The librarian, a woman much older than my mother, finally looked over at me.

"Can I help you young man?" she said just above a whisper.

I held up my library card for her to see.

"Yes," she said, "very nice."

"I need a book about going to the Moon," I said a little too loudly for her liking.

She placed a finger to her lips.

"Well, let's see what we can find," she said softly as she got up and led me past a few stacks. We arrived at the *Science* section next to the ladies room, where she moved along a shelf then back along the one below it before stopping.

"Here," she whispered, "is a very famous one by a man named

Jules Verne."

She handed it to me.

Then in a voice a little less subdued she said, "Oh, and here's one that's even more recent,"

It was The Conquest of Space by Willey Ley.

It had a spaceship on the cover that was taking off *from* the Moon. It was already there! I was hooked.

"Can I take them both," I asked, already looking at the pictures in one of them.

"They must be returned in two weeks. Can you read them both by then?" was her reply.

A more appropriate question would have been "*is there any chance you won't have read them both with a flashlight under the covers before dawn tomorrow?*"

The nuns at Saint John's didn't exactly prevent me from learning science but ultimately it became an exercise in self-teaching. I even talked my parents into getting me a subscription to Scientific American magazine. It was generally over my head but I loved the pictures and longed to do some of the experiments I saw in its pages. I remember Mom discouraging my feeble, baking soda rocket engine research project in the kitchen sink.

"Do you know what you're doing?" she worried, "You could put your eye out."

"Oh Ma, it just makes carbon dioxide gas," I said.

I guess that convinced her because she walked away, declaring, "Then be sure to clean up that mess when you're done."

The week before Christmas 1955, while my parents were out and after a thorough search of the house, I discovered a good sized cardboard box under their bed. I was sure it was the chemistry set I longed for but on Christmas morning I could hardly keep my disappointment from showing.

There was no chemistry set. No dissolving pennies in nitric acid, no hydrogen sulfide stink bombs, no chance to continue Newton's experiments trying to turn lead into gold at my little basement work bench; instead, they gave me a kit to make a one tube radio.

You've got to be kidding, I thought, *What am I going to do with this?*

By nightfall my disappointment had vanished as I listened to music from Chicago, anti-American propaganda from Moscow and ham radio operators talking and sending Morse code from as far away as Europe. I couldn't get enough. Thoughts of chemistry slipped away as radio and electricity filled my every waking hour. I learned Morse code with a Radio Shack key and buzzer, got every possible cub scout radio merit badge, studied FCC manuals and finally after what seemed like years-- because it <u>was</u> years-- I felt ready to take the general class amateur radio license test. It would allow me to use all the ham radio bands and up to one thousand watts of power, but first I had to send and receive Morse code at thirteen words per minute and pass a written test on electronic theory.

It was 1957 and I was ready. So dressed in my best coat and tie, I took the bus and subway to the Customs House in Boston. When I stepped off the elevator on the 15th floor, there were seven other applicants sitting at desks facing the FCC examiner.

He told me to take a seat and then said, "Okay we're all here now so please put on the headphones located at your desk. I'm going to send 5 minutes of plain text. You have to copy one minute perfectly to pass. Pencils ready..."

I was nervous but somehow managed to copy the one minute needed then we moved on to the written test.

The examiner handed out the booklets and said, "Make sure your name and address are on the answer sheet. You have one hour. Good luck."

After twenty-five minutes I approached the desk.

The examiner looked up, "Yes?" he queried.

"I finished," I said, holding up my exam paper.

"Put it here on the desk. We'll let you know," he said with an automatic grin.

I set it down in front of him as he went back to reading his magazine.

I didn't move. He looked up and put the magazine down.

"Yes? What is it?" he asked.

"I'm finished with the exam."

"I can see that. You'll hear from us," he said with a touch of irritation in his voice.

He picked up the magazine, found his place and continued reading.

I didn't move, but watched as his eyes went down the page. Then he noticed me again and glanced over the magazine.

"What?" he said, "I just--" At that point, I guess he figured out that there wasn't much chance of me moving.

"Oh, all right. I'll take a look," he said.

He put the magazine aside and picked up my exam. With a pencil he traced his way from top to bottom of the answer sheet comparing it to the one laying on his desk.

"There!" he said looking up, "Happy? You passed. You're all set," he announced.

"Can I operate as a general class ham now?" I asked.

He looked up toward the ceiling and said, "Not until you receive the license in the mail."

"How long will that take?" I asked, not trying to hide my disappointment.

"This all has to get sent to Washing--", We made eye contact. His face softened. "Okay. Wait," he said, opening the top drawer of the desk. He took out a printed pink pad, wrote a few things on the top form, signed it, tore it off and handed it to me. "Here you go," he said, "A temporary operators license. Good until yours comes in the mail. Now go."

"Gee thanks," I said, heading for the elevator.

My dad had helped me put up antennas and I had already built a transmitter in anticipation of this day, so when I got home I was *on the air* for real. I was nervous but I "talked" to an amateur radio operator in Belgium that night using Morse code!

My dad worked at Hanscom Air Force Base as a *procurement officer* (whatever that was) and had a co-worker, Joe Mammola who took an interest in me after I accompanied Dad to a *'take your kid to work'* event. He was an electrical engineer at MIT Lincoln Labs and got me radio parts and gave me advice for my projects. (In fact, he had recommended the one tube radio kit that my father gave me that Christmas.) He helped me get my starting jobs in electronics and it was Joe who suggested to my dad years later that I should apply to MIT.

Summer was approaching and I learned the hard way, that to

avoid endless chores around the house, I would have to convince my father that I was too busy to do them.

On the first day of school vacation, my dad poked his head into my room at 7:00 AM and said, "Okay, time to get up!"

At my Ham Radio Station (1957)

Without carefully considering my response, I replied from under the covers, "I don't have to get up. There's nothing I have to do today."

I don't know what I was thinking but dad's comeback was instantaneous, "Fine. Then I'll leave you a list of things to do. You'll find it on the kitchen table and be sure they're done before I get home."

The list involved mowing, cutting, sweeping, shoveling, hauling and painting. And that was just the morning!

That's when I realized that I needed a summer job. But being thirteen, what job could I get?

Joe Mammola to the rescue again. He heard of my plight and took me to meet Antonari Tassinari, the owner of *Day Square Radio-TV Repair* in East Boston. Tass (as he was called) showed some interest as I described the radio station and workbench I had in my basement at home. He liked to tell jokes, was easy to talk to and seemed impressed that I knew one end of a vacuum tube from the other. Right then and there, he hired me... at 25 cents an hour. Beginning the next day I followed him around the store and he showed me the ropes and a few tricks of the trade (including how *not* to get electrocuted while working on a TV that had a 5000 volt power supply.)

The lessons weren't just technical.

"The first thing to learn is to ask the right questions," he said.

Now he impersonated a customer and using a falsetto voice said, "*My car radio sometimes doesn't work.*"

Then he answered as himself, "Oh... when doesn't it work, ma'am?"

And again as the customer, "*When I go through the tunnel under the harbor.*"

We both laughed.

"Be sure to ask the right questions before you start," he concluded.

"But what would I tell her?" I asked.

"Tell her... stay out of the tunnel," he replied.

We both laughed again. The lessons continued.

"The next thing you do is see if there's current getting through the power cord," he told me. He took his index finger and placed it across the power terminals of a radio on the bench. "Whoa," he uttered as he pulled the finger back quickly, "...there's power there all right. The cord is fine."

I stood with my mouth open.

He looked at me and said, "Of course... *you*... you would use the volt meter."

The next day he asked me, "Do you believe in the law of averages?"

"I do," I answered.

"So how come in all the years I've been doing this, not once has a television worked without being plugged in?"

"I don't know," I replied, a little confused.

"See! You don't know everything. Remember that," he said.

"I will," I said. (*And I have.*)

Soon I got my own work space with my own soldering iron and my own oscilloscope. I got pretty good at fixing radios and TVs but found my forte was working on car radios. To fix them (and they often broke in 1957) it was necessary to remove them from the dashboard, which required a small person (namely me) upside down, twisting, squeezing and contorting to fit in an incredibly small space. That first summer I spent a lot of time under people's dashboards.

But it wasn't all great fun; in fact, I had a problem. To get to the shop, I took a bus from near my house to Orient Heights, then the Blue line train to Day Square station. This all cost 40 cents-- one way! And lunch at Georgie Porgie's Diner was another 75 cents. So by the time I took the subway home it cost me $1.55 to earn $2.00! Three weeks in, I confronted Tass at his work bench.

"Excuse me Mr. Tassinari," I said, when there were no customers in the front of the repair shop.

"Call me Tass," he replied while fiddling with an Emerson 5 tube table radio chassis.

"Do you think I could have a raise, Mr. Tassinari?"

Now he gave me his full attention.

"A raise? How much am I paying you now?" he asked.

"Twenty five cents," I answered; quickly adding, "an hour."

He looked me up and down and said, "I'm losing money on you now."

He didn't wait for any reaction but continued, "Do you know who you should feel sorry for?"

I shrugged then leaned against the bench; my legs having become very tired.

"I'll tell you, " he said, "The poor guy who makes two hundred dollars a week, that's who!"

"Why?" I questioned.

"Because if he gets sick and misses two days work, he loses eighty dollars! You? You would only lose..." he screwed up his face indicating math taking place in his brain, "...four dollars! Isn't that better than losing eighty? Huh?" He had a really satisfied look on his face and turned his attention back to the radio set he had been working on.

Then without looking up from his chore he said, "How does seventy five cents an hour sound?"

"Do you mean it?" I said excitedly as my legs (with their strength slowly returning) carried me over to my own work bench.

"That doesn't start until tomorrow though," he added, "...And call me Tass."

"Thank you, thank you, Mr. Tassinari!" I said.

I learned a lot there. I learned how to tell the manufacture date on a vacuum tube. If *859183* was stenciled on the glass (in very tiny print) I could tell you it was made the week of September 15, 1958. And the best part was that I was one of the few people that knew the secret (and it came in handy when people tried to return an old tube as new!)

I learned how to incapacitate flies (and there were a lot of flies in the workshop) with the pressurized carbon dioxide gas we used to clean electronic parts. I'm reluctant to admit that they often met an unpleasant end at my hands while they were groggy.

One day, Tass asked me, "How do you know the light really goes out in the refrigerator when you close the door?"

"Of course it does," I replied.

"How do you know?"

"Because I... you see... well as you close...", I faltered and gave up.

"See! Don't be so sure of everything," he chided me.

The next day I came in to work with five or six different ways you could tell if the light really went out. The ideas ranged from electric circuits with photo cells, to automatic cameras, to volunteer midget observers in parkas. He seemed pleased with them all.

I worked there six days a week all summer and every Saturday during the school year until I entered MIT in the fall of 1962. When I left I was making $7.50 an hour. Electronic appliances back then were not nearly as dependable as now and broke down often, but... they could be fixed.

And it was a really great feeling that I was someone who could fix them.

The Strangler

"Hey Ma, what's all the commotion up on Banks Street?" I asked after arriving home from school, "It looks like every police car in town is up there."

"Aunt Tina said they've been there for hours," she answered.

It was only four-thirty but being December, darkness was settling in and the blue flashing lights were hard to ignore.

"I'm going up there and see what I can find out," I said as I pulled my coat back on.

"Be back by five for supper. You know how your father hates to wait."

I walked the six houses up and there was even more going on than I had thought. The police were there of course, as well as news reporters, a medical examiner's van, cameramen... and one of the cars had *Suffolk County District Attorney's Office* stenciled on the side.

All of the activity seemed to be centered at the Monihan's house. *Probably that stupid dog*, I thought.

Their German Shepherd was always out front, chained to the porch and tried to attack anyone who walked by. His chain kept him about two inches from the white picket fence so the neighborhood kids would stick their finger though the slats to tease him as they passed by on the sidewalk. I always figured his bark was worse than his bite... but maybe not, judging from all the police.

The Monihans had two kids; Margaret, a year younger than me and in the eleventh grade, and Thomas about twelve years old. I hardly ever saw Tommy, but Margaret was always friendly and we would often stop and talk on the street. She went to a private Catholic school in the next town so I didn't really know her that well. She wasn't particularly pretty but she was the only girl who ever showed an interest in my radio hobby and I could tell she liked me. Last November, she greeted me on the

Margaret (1962)

sidewalk while I was walking past her house.

She wasted no time and began, "Hi. There's a dance at my school, the Friday before Thanksgiving and I was wondering if you'd like to go with me."

"At your school?" I said to buy time, "that would be the... eighteenth ... right?"

"Seventeenth," she corrected.

The thought of going to a dance, any dance, didn't excite me but I had to give her an answer and not wanting to hurt her feelings, I said "Sure, that would be great."

She told me a little about the dance and then I said awkwardly, "Well... I have to get home. So I'll see you at seven on the... "

"Seventeenth," she said.

I walked home wondering how I got myself into these things and to make matters worse, the next day my friends, as I expected, gave me a hard time about it.

"I guess you're kinda hard up since Tami told you to take a hike," chided Paul.

"Oh Margaret, I think I love you," Al Coleman said while wrapping his arms around himself and making kissing noises.

"What's the matter with you?" I said, "She's nice enough... and it's kinda flattering--"

But they wouldn't let it go.

So finally I said, "Cut it out! It's none of your damn business anyway. I'm taking her to a dance and... if you don't like it... that's tough!"

That was the best I could come up with, and of course, I still wasn't looking forward to it, but part of me (the vain part) didn't mind a girl (any girl) thinking I was cool. So I figured I'd give it my best shot and surprisingly, once I began thinking that way, I felt a little more comfortable about the whole thing.

Maybe it won't be so bad, I thought.

I bought a corsage, drove up to her house in my dad's Mercury and stood at the gate as the dog attempted to reach me while barking his head off. Tommy came out, shouted something and the dog walked up onto the porch, tail between its legs, looking terrified and sat.

"You can come in now, if you want," he said, "but Meg's not

ready."

I talked to Mrs. Monihan for a few minutes then Margaret came down the stairs with her hair all done up and she was wearing a blue dress. I don't think I had ever seen her not wearing a school uniform before.

Not bad, I thought.

As we walked out to the car she called back to her mom, "Be sure Pal is inside before we get home."

The dog's name is Pal *!* I thought to myself, *What would they have named him if he was friendly?*

The dance was in a gymnasium decorated to look like a Pilgrim village. There were cut-out drawings of Pilgrim hats and turkeys, a large mural of the Mayflower at anchor and lots and lots of pumpkins. I didn't know anyone else there but we slow-danced a bit, snacked a bit and talked a bit. Margaret introduced me to a few nuns and some of her friends and showed me around the school grounds. I never really felt comfortable but she was easy enough to be with and appeared to be enjoying herself. I drove her home and without the dog on the porch, we managed an awkward *thank you for a nice evening* good night kiss. It might have been a little better if I didn't have to listen to Pal feverishly barking upstairs.

Margaret opened the front door.

"Thanks," she said over the sound of the barking, "I had a good time."

"No; thank *you*," I replied, always the gentleman.

"Good night... " she said. Then just before she closed the door, "...you can call me if you like."

"Okay," I said without conviction.

Well, that wasn't so bad, I thought as I drove down the street and parked the Mercury in the driveway. With the holiday and all, I didn't see her for the next couple of weeks and I never bothered to call her.

. . .

The blue lights weren't flashing anymore and most of the official looking cars were leaving. Two uniformed policemen were setting up wooden barricades with ropes between them to block the entrance to the property.

I went up to a man carrying an impressive camera with a large flashbulb rig attached and asked, "What's going on?"

"You can read it in tomorrow's paper," he joked, but then he got serious, "Someone was attacked. Boston strangler maybe... but they're not sure."

He walked off.

"How serious?" I called after him.

"Pretty serious. It seems there was a fatality," he yelled back without turning around.

I shouted, "Who?" but got no reply.

The people out on the sidewalk didn't know any more than I did. Rumors abounded. Boston Strangler in my town? On my street? My God, lock your doors!

Someone had seen a covered stretcher carried out but didn't know who it was.

Then... Al, who lived a few doors up, said he heard that the cops had taken Tommy in a paddy wagon about an hour ago...

I didn't sleep much that night. In the morning, the Boston papers had the story. The news wasn't good.

It had been a Catholic holy day; no school for the Monihan kids. At noontime, while the parents were at work, Tommy had called the police and reported that a man had come into the house and attacked his sister while he, Tom, hid in a closet. The attacker had nearly decapitated Margaret! The police at first assumed possibly the Boston Strangler was afoot but nothing really fit. Then while interviewing neighbors, a detective realized that no one had heard Pal bark around that time. Not a whimper.

So... no barking, meant... no intruder, which meant... Tommy.

He confessed. Apparently they had a fight over what station to play on the radio so he strangled her, stabbed her and then stuffed her nearly severed head in a pot of water.

Because he was under-age, the story dried up. People in the neighborhood felt better, of course, because it wasn't the Boston Strangler... just Tommy.

But Margaret was dead. And I know it wouldn't have made any difference but... I wish I had called her.

Falling for Donna

The week after graduating high school, I was an usher at my sister wedding and before setting off on their honeymoon, my new brother-in-law, Bill asked me if I'd like to use his car (a green and white, 1955 Ford) while they were away. He had let me drive it many times while courting my sister as a means of getting me out of the house.

I had been accepted to MIT, was working days at a TV repair shop (so I had some spending money) and now was offered a car to cruise to the beach on the warm summer evenings... who could pass that up. I jumped at the chance, despite the car having a problem. The passenger side door was almost impossible to unlatch but had a tendency to unexpectedly fly open while the car was moving. That, coupled with the fact that back then, cars had no seat belts, made driving with a girl in the front seat, not only difficult but rather dangerous. Bill had adopted the only logical (if not elegant) solution; a rope connecting the passenger's side door handle with the driver's side door handle. An added benefit was that it acted a little like a seat belt as it passed in front of the occupants. Entering and exiting the vehicle was a bit complicated but after all... the car *was* free.

So on a warm night in early July, I picked up my friend, Al, and drove to Winthrop Beach to sit on the four-foot high seawall, already crowded with our high school friends. The wall ran the entire length of the beach below, but we all congregated at one spot where there was an opening with steps that led down to the sand. It was all very lively and driven by one simple desire; the boys wanted to be where the girls were and the girls wanted to be where the boys were. It was the 1962 small town version of social media.

I definitely wanted to be with girls but felt a little awkward around them. It was much easier with other boys nearby and the wall provided a place to flirt with the girls while we tried to figure out what we were expected to do next. (It didn't occur to me at the time that once I started college in two months, I would never see most of them again.)

My eighteenth birthday was approaching and I was almost totally under the influence of hormones as evidenced by acne and a nearly permanent erection. My steady girlfriend all through high school was, due to a combination of ineptitude and immaturity on my part, not speaking to me and as fate would have it, the two other girls that I had recently dated weren't there that night.

I was watching the planes out over the ocean lined up to land at Logan Airport when Al walked over. He considered hoisting his pudgy frame up onto the wall but then thought better of it.

"You see that girl over there?" he said, motioning with his head, "Her boyfriend never showed up tonight so I told her you'd give her a ride home."

"Thanks a lot," I said sarcastically... but then I looked up and saw her.

She had dark hair and very blue eyes accented by the street light shining above.

"Cute," I said under my breath and hopped down to the sidewalk.

"Listen, I'll pick you up later," I told him quietly just as the girl approached.

"Al said you might give me a ride home."

"I don't believe we've met. I don't even know your name," I said.

At this point it gets interesting because I *thought* she said, "My name is Mary Kelly."

"Okay," I said, "Now that we've met, I can drive you home."

We walked to the car and I opened the driver's door for her. She hesitated for just an instant but needed the ride, so she slid over on the bench seat to the passenger side, avoiding the rope. I slid in then pulled the rope taut and tied a knot of some kind.

"You can drop me off at the corner of Somerset Ave and I'll walk to my house. My parents don't allow me to accept rides from boys," she informed me.

I didn't know what to make of her, she was so straight forward... and young... and cute.

The AM radio was tuned to WMEX. A fifties oldie was playing, so I turned up the volume.

"Del Vikings," I said, "1956," showing off.

I couldn't tell if she was impressed or not.

When we arrived at the corner, I untied the rope (trying to look as cool as possible while undoing a granny knot), got out and let her slide over and out. Then I got back in.

"Good night," I said, out the window of the '55 Ford.

"Thank you," she said.

I watched her walk away.

Too bad she has a boyfriend, I thought, then re-tied the rope and drove back to the beach.

1955 Ford: How could she resist?

There was a bigger crowd now than before.

I found Al.

"That girl. Who is she? What's she like?" I asked.

"I dunno," he answered, "I don't know her that well. I think she's in the ninth grade."

"Ninth grade?" I repeated, "But she's going into the tenth, right?"

I questioned a few more of my friends.

"Hey, what do you know about Mary Kelly?" I asked.

"Mary Kelly? I don't know any Mary Kelly," or "Never heard of her," were typical responses.

"Damn!," I said aloud, "She gave me a fake name, then makes me drop her off at a corner so I won't know where she lives. Can you beat that?"

"What are you talking about?" one of the group asked.

"Nothing. I'm just an idiot, that's all," I replied for everyone to hear.

No one appeared to disagree.

A week later on a hot sunny day, I was sitting on the wall and who did I see walking on the beach? Mary Kelly; that's who.

So I kicked off my shoes and ran down the beach. The sand was hot on my feet as I came up behind her.

I tapped her on the shoulder and said, "Hello... *Mary*."

She turned with a surprised look on her face and said, "Oh... hi..."

She appeared to be a bit confused.

"Mary Kelly. That is your name isn't it?" I said.

"No," she said. "It's Donna. Donna Marukelli."

"Oh," I said sheepishly.

I didn't see any nearby holes to crawl into so I began trying to explain. But I found her so attractive at that moment, I suddenly forgot about false names, boyfriends and even likely rejection.

"Do you want to go out on Saturday?" I heard myself ask, "To a movie or something?"

Of course, I didn't know it then but my destiny would be determined by her answer.

"Yes, I'd love to," she said.

"Great. I'll pick you up at seven," I said. "...Hey, wait a minute. Where do you live?"

She gave me her address and we parted. I walked back to get my shoes, repeating her address over and over so I wouldn't forget it and no longer noticed the hot sand.

At seven on Saturday I was greeted at the door by Donna's mother.

"She'll be ready in a minute," she said, "Come in. Have a seat."

She pointed to the sofa. I sat down and the lights flickered, so I quickly stood up and they went back on.

"Oh, they always do that," she said.

I moved the couch slightly and the lights flickered.

"Would you like me to fix this?" I asked, "Do you have a screwdriver handy?"

Mrs. Marukelli (who I soon learned was called Mimi) brought me the oldest, most beat-up screwdriver I had ever seen. It's split wooden handle was held together with electrical tape. I moved the couch, rewired the plug on a lamp cord, reconfigured three multi-tap outlet adapters with a myriad of extension cords then moved the couch back and sat down gingerly. The lights stayed on. Mimi and I were friends for life.

Donna and I went to perhaps the worst date movie ever made-- <u>Judgment At Nuremberg</u>. Afterward we stopped at Hamm's Deli where I hoped to salvage the evening over a chocolate soda and while talking we discovered we had a mutual friend.

"I was at her New Years Eve party," I said, "I went with Bunny Luongo but what I remember most was a girl across the room wearing purple ski pants."

I made what some might have interpreted as a lewd gesture.

"Who was she?" Donna asked as if perhaps she might know her.

" I don't know. I didn't get a look at her face."

Donna got a coy expression and began, "I was there... and guess what I was wearing?"

"Purple ski pants?" I exclaimed, "Oh my god... that was you?"

I had no idea how things were going but I felt that I might perhaps be going down in flames.

Does she thinks that's a compliment or that I'm a jerk? I wondered.

The more I tried to impress her, the more I was sure that the night was not going well... until I drove her home and walked her to the door. I surely didn't know much about girls but I did know that the good night kiss would tell me what I needed to know about my chances and as much as I looked forward to it, I was dreading it. What if she didn't like me and gave me that little "thanks for a nice evening" light peck on the lips. I thought some of my previous girlfriends had been pretty good kissers and I enjoyed making out with them but that night on the porch under a thoughtfully sized 15 watt bulb, my perspective changed forever. Our first kiss was a game changer. She leaned in and kissed me like she meant it and I wanted more; so I immediately asked her out on another date.

S*he's something...* I thought as I drove home, *...I wonder who her boyfriend is.*

Dominic Martucci owned a new, red Pontiac Bonneville convertible and how fortunate for me that he had failed to pick up Donna at the wall that night. He hadn't graduated yet and worked for his father's rendering business driving a truck and picking up bones at local restaurants. Three of his friends stopped me one night at the wall to tell me how unhappy he was that I had dated his girl.

"I'm sorry he's unhappy," I said, "but it's up to her who she dates."

"Things could happen to you, you know," one of them said.

Another chimed in, "like you could fall off this wall."

We all looked down at the water below.

Winthrop was a small town, and it was 1962, so those words only evoked the following response from me, "I think you've been watching too many gangster movies."

I hopped down from the wall to the pavement, walked away and repeated, "It's up to her."

I never did meet Dominic, so I can only guess that he agreed.

Oh, and by the way, the fall from the wall to the water... at that point, was at most... five feet.

MIT

There's something about walking into the principal's office-- even if you're not being disciplined-- that makes you feel uneasy; especially if that principal is Mr. Duplin. At the high school we referred to him as *the snake* due to his ability to slither unnoticed into a classroom and suddenly pounce on student wrongdoers.

But I needed his recommendation for my college application, so I rapped on his door and waited to hear, "Come in." He was sitting at his cluttered desk.

"What can I do for you?... Ernest, is it?" he asked.

I hadn't been in enough trouble that he could easily remember my name. In fact, my last run-in with him was months ago when I wrote a short story in Miss McIntyre's Creative Writing English class. It was about an English teacher named Miss Pleez-Retyre.

I was sent down to the principal's office where Mr. Duplin told me, "If you don't apologize to her immediately, you will be punished."

I tried to explain that it was just a work of fiction but he didn't buy it.

"Apology or suspension. Your choice," he said, "Which is it?"

I apologized. (But I didn't mean it.)

So now I was explaining that I needed his letter of recommendation for my MIT application and that the deadline was January 15th. He looked at me standing there, then at his desk piled with papers, then back at me.

"What makes you think you could get into MIT?" he asked.

I shrugged my shoulders and said. "I don't know... my dad wants me to apply."

"But you're not going to get in," he said. Then he stood. "Let me show you something."

He walked over to a cabinet and found a file.

"Do you know who Joe Palasko is?" he asked.

"Sure," I said.

Everyone knew of Joe. Star of last year's championship football team, captain of the debate team, good looking, king of the senior prom, *blah, blah, blah.* Mr. Duplin held the file out to me. I stayed where I was.

"Do you see this?" he asked rhetorically. "Honor roll. A's only. Accepted into the Naval Academy." Now Mr. Duplin changed to a more fatherly tone. "He applied to MIT... and wasn't accepted. Now, why do you think you have a chance?"

"My father wants me to apply," I repeated.

He tried another tack.

Sweeping his hand over the pile of files on his desk he said, "Look at these. All requests for letters of recommendation. It will take me a month to get through them." He pointed to one and continued, "This one is for Phyllis Cohen. She's applying to Simmons. Just what they need; another Jew."

I expected a bolt of lightning to strike the room and I wanted to get out before it did.

"I really have to go," I said, "I'll... I'll leave this form on your desk."

I stepped back.

"You're wasting your money," he said as I opened the door.

"My dad's paying and he wants me to apply," I said from the hall. Then under my breath, *You obviously don't know my dad.*

I figured I'd get accepted to Tufts and RPI for sure, so there was no harm in one more application for the hell of it. (And besides, did I mention that my dad wanted me to apply.)

I also asked my twelfth grade math teacher, Mr. Brontus Martus to write me a recommendation letter. He was working on his math PHD at MIT at the time and he liked me because I helped him draw the graphs that showed the relationship between Moire patterns and some obscure equations for his thesis.

"What exactly is this good for?" I asked him one day.

"That's the beauty of math," he said, "It doesn't have to be good for anything."

I really didn't expect to get in to MIT which might explain why, when on January 14th my sister asked me, "Did you have your interview at MIT yet," I answered, "Uh... no."

Her stare, and my guilt pushed me into action.

I called the admission office at 4:30 in the afternoon and told them who I was, then asked, "Can I arrange for an interview?"

"All the interviewers have left," she said, "Tomorrow *is* the last day you know. Let me put you on hold."

When she came back on the line she said, "If you can come in tomorrow before noon, Mr. Greeley could interview you then."

I said I would and the next morning I put on a sport coat and tie, drove to Cambridge, parked on Mass Avenue, found my way to building 7 and located the admissions office. On the door was stenciled, *Horace B. Greeley, Director of Admissions.* I sat waiting for a few minutes then was called into his office.

Now this is some office, I thought.

Everything about it was impressive. Big sunny windows, plants, books, diplomas everywhere, really nice furniture and a bust of Galileo.

"Have a seat," said Mr. Greeley, "Tell me what you like to do after school each day."

I told him about the educational stuff that I did after school and left out most of the rest. Then the interview got tougher.

"Who wrote your high school chemistry book?" he asked.

I wanted to say, "You're kidding, right?" but instead I said, "I don't know."

Then he asked about hobbies and I told him about my amateur radio station.

"What about stamp collecting?" he asked.

"Stamp collecting? Talk about dull... who would do that?" I said.

If I had been looking carefully at him as I spoke, I would have seen him stiffen slightly in his chair.

"I do," he said.

"Oh... well... it could be fun, I bet," I said. *Tufts here I come,* I thought.

When I got the MIT acceptance letter in April, all I could think of was that the admissions committee saw that their boss had interviewed me personally and they figured they had better let me in; or Mr. Duplin had a change of heart and wrote a really persuasive letter; or Mr. Martus had more pull at MIT than I imagined; or I suppose, you can't rule out... my Uncle Sal.

In any case, in September 1962, I went from being one of the smartest kids in Winthrop High School-- without even really trying-- to being the only kid at MIT that couldn't figure out what the hell the instructors were talking about. My calculus lecturer wrote on the chalkboard with his right hand while simultaneously erasing with his left. Nothing stayed visible for more than 15 seconds! And we were marked on a curve, so giving help to a classmate only lowered your own grade.

But I was lucky enough to live in a great fraternity house. SAE fraternity on Beacon Street gave me friends, help, confidence and a social life. It was a combination of family and (on the weekends) Animal House. My fraternity brothers during those years became among other things: the first astronaut to space-walk from the NASA shuttle, a congressman, a circus doctor and a DJ at a Cleveland radio station.

I struggled with math, loved electrical engineering and computer science and comprehended physics (before quantum physics, that is) pretty well. It was an amazing education in so many ways. I learned to think like an engineer and left my boyhood (if reluctantly) behind. It was not easy but I managed to get through it. (I did need an extra term... but that's another story.)

So I graduated in January 1967 with my fraternity brother, Fred Souk, who was a political science major and originally in the class of '65 (another long story.) He and I walked over to the bursar's office together, where they checked our accounts to see that all bills were paid (and that I had finally passed my swimming test!) and handed us our diplomas.

We walked out of the bursar's office, stood together in the hallway in building 7, where Fred stuck out his hand to me and said, "Congratulations my friend; but... it did take you four and a half years. I, on the other hand, was able to do it in... *five* and a half years," then he took a bow.

When anyone asks me who the commencement speaker at my MIT graduation was, I tell them... Fred Souk.

Paul

I held out the money and showed it to my friend Paul Clancy.

"Twenty-two dollars... and fifty cents," I said, "all since I got the raise at the TV repair shop."

"What are you gonna do with it?" he asked.

I got the feeling that he had some ideas (probably involving lemon squares and Coca-Colas at Brother's Bakery.)

"I'm going to open a savings account," I declared, "My dad says I can use my new FCC radio license as identification."

"Savings account... what for?" he asked.

"For college." I said.

Paul's response was quick and to the point, "College? My dad says college is a waste of time." Then when that didn't seem to have the desired effect, he tried, "Besides, you won't be going to college for at least five years! There may not even be colleges then."

I had to admit he had a good argument but I was determined, and we set out for Winthrop Center, somehow made it past the bakery and arrived at the bank. (Picture *Bailey's Savings and Loan* from *It's a Wonderful Life*.) Old Mrs. Cashman called me to her window.

"How can I help you young man?" she asked in her high-pitched voice.

"I want to open a savings account, please," I replied and handed her the money and my radio license.

She slowly made her way to a desk behind her and with a lot of clickety-clacking produced a passbook. The dollar amounts and dates were not just printed in ink but embossed permanently on the pages. She came back to the window and handed the brand new passbook to me.

"Be sure to spend it wisely," she said.

Paul was behind me, quietly mimicking her squeaky voice, "Be sure to spend it on lemon squares, young man."

We stepped out onto the sidewalk and I studied my new treasure. The FCC allowed an operator's address and a station's address to be different, but in my case, since they were the same, printed across the top where it said location, was SAME AS BELOW. So of course, Mrs. Cashman had made my savings account in the name of Sam Asbelow!

It took quite a while to cancel Mr. Asbelow's account and transfer his money to me but Mrs. Cashman eventually managed to do it. But as hard as I tried that summer, I could not get Paul to stop calling me Sam.

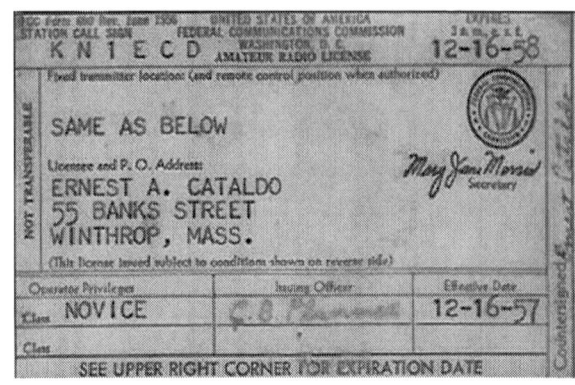

Sam Asbelow's ID

. . .

Paul lived two doors up from me on Banks Street but I'm not exactly sure what his house looked like, as it was hidden by enormous untrimmed bushes and tall uncut grass. The porch was piled with broken furniture, a rusty baby carriage, a push lawnmower, trash barrels and a refrigerator. Even on Halloween, kids avoided the place. It was just Paul and his dad that lived there. (His mother lived somewhere up north. She apparently was smart enough to get out while she could.) I had no idea what Paul's dad did for a living; he kept funny hours and rarely spoke to any of us.

One Friday afternoon, Paul came to my door and asked, "Do want to come with my dad and me? We're going out to supper and then shoplifting for pants tonight in Boston."

"What?"

"Yeah, Dad's great at it. We have this system where you take three pairs into the--"

"Wait a minute," I whispered as I stepped out onto the porch and pulled the door behind me, "You're going to shoplift pants?"

"Sure," he said, "You don't want to come?"

"Well... no... not tonight," I said trying to process what I was hearing, "Thanks for asking though."

"Suit yourself," he said, "See you tomorrow."

The only time I ever had a one-on-one conversation with Mr. Clancy was one summer morning when I was fourteen. He saw me passing his house and motioned for me to come on to the porch. I made my way cautiously up the steps.

"Were you at the beach yesterday morning when Paul fell off that rock?" he asked.

"Yes sir," I replied, "But I didn't-- "

"I know, don't worry. I'd like you to go to the Winthrop Hospital Emergency room with Paul and tell them he just fell off the rock... *this* morning."

Paul came out onto the porch. He wasn't wearing a shirt and his arm was in a makeshift sling made from a well used dishtowel. He wasn't smiling. I could see his bare arm was puffed up and blue and yellow and...

"Yikes! That's gross" I exclaimed.

Paul lamented, "I told him it was broken but he never--"

Mr. Clancy interrupted, "Will you just do what I ask? Go there now."

We set off to the hospital; a twenty minute walk.

"What's going on?" I asked.

"I couldn't sleep all night," he said, "This hurts!"

"No, I mean why do I have to say--"

"My dad says our insurance won't cover this because I didn't go right to the hospital yesterday," he explained, "So... you're my witness. It happened this morning. Okay?"

I'm the worst liar in the world and I always have been, so at the hospital when the doctor began examining Paul, he looked at me and said skeptically, "When did you say this fall occurred?"

I froze and my face began reddening. I kept silent.

"It didn't happen today, did it?" he said a little louder.

I remained immobile and went crimson.

Paul was in such pain he wasn't aware that I was about to let him down.

"Is this about insurance? Because if it is, don't worry about that. I need to know when this happened," the doctor said earnestly.

"Yesterday morning!" I blurted out without hesitation.

"Thank you," the doctor said.

We were there until mid-afternoon. They gave Paul a hard cast and a real sling and then we walked back home.

Paul appeared to be high from the pain killers they had given him. He held up a pill bottle and asked, "You want one? They're great man."

"That's okay," I said, "I'll pass."

Paul told me later that when his dad came home that evening and heard how the day went, he wanted to break his other arm.

Paul didn't seem to care that I had been unable to lie. Maybe he figured out that it was actually better for him that I told the doctor the truth. It was a complicated friendship.

Paul was quick witted, usually funny but occasionally sad.

He borrowed money from me and was quick to say, "Don't worry, it will all even out in the end."

Well, *in the end*, he and his dad abruptly moved away one night. I received a letter a few months later in which he acknowledged that he owed me a lot of money, said he was sorry and wished me luck. They had moved to L.A.

. . .

My friends, Paul & Al (1960)

Four years later, during a college break, I decided to visit my old high school pal. I shared the driving with Mike Mednick, a fraternity brother, as we cruised west along the soon to be obsolete Route 66. We endured a night in Warsaw, Indiana and a hail storm (with hail stones the size of golf balls) near Amarillo, Texas. On the third day, the Mercury Comet we were driving, began to act up. We stopped and found a Ford repair garage in Ponca City, Oklahoma and had a mechanic look under the hood.

"Yup, it's your distributor alright," he said, "she's cooked."

"Do you have one?" Mike asked hopefully.

"Well, wish I did... but I don't," he said, "We can get one delivered tomorrow morning though, before ten... if you'd like."

Next day after eating breakfast in our roadside motel, we walked back to the garage and there was a small knot of people milling around.

"What's happening?" I asked one of them.

"I heard the Greyhound bus is stopping in town this morning," he said, "Thought I'd come down and see for myself."

Sure enough the bus turned down the street off the highway and stopped. With the engine still running, the driver got out, opened the luggage door and held up a package.

"That'll be for me," the mechanic said as he stepped forward and retrieved it.

The bus departed, the dust settled and the small crowd soon dispersed.

An hour later the mechanic took the Comet out for a test drive.

As the car was being parked in front of the garage, Mike said to me, "What do ya think this will cost?"

"I don't know," I said, "but it's not like you have any choice."

The mechanic left the engine running, walked over to us and announced, "She's all set. Good as new. That'll be thirty-seven fifty."

Mike glanced at me, smiled and held out two twenties.

"Keep the change," he said and we were soon back on Route 66.

"That felt like a Twilight Zone episode" I said as we picked up speed.

Mike just kept smiling.

It was 1:30 AM before we had crossed the desert and arrived in Seal Beach, California where I was dropped off in front of a run-down one story structure, set on pilings, that looked more like a fishing shack than a house. I took out the crumpled letter and double-checked the address just to be sure.

"I guess this is it," I said as I pulled my suitcase out of the back seat, "see you back in Boston."

Mike looked around then said, "Good luck," rolled up the window and quickly drove off toward his home in Downey.

I could hear and smell the ocean as I walked up onto the porch, opened the screen door and found a note taped to the inner door.

With the help of the street light out at the sidewalk, It read:

> Ernie- Paul asked me to tell you that he's in jail. He says to find a place to sleep and he'll try to meet you here tomorrow afternoon.

"Find a place to sleep?" I muttered, "You gotta be kidding me!" Being desperate, I tried the door but it was locked.

I went out to the street with my suitcase and began to walk toward some lights. One minute later a car pulled up next to me and the most professional looking policeman I had ever seen, looked out the window and said. "Can I be of some help, sir?"

All his buttons were polished and fastened and he was wearing a gleaming white plastic helmet.

Toto, we're not in Boston anymore, I thought.

I explained the situation and he got on the radio, then said, "Your friend was arrested last night for indecent exposure. He'll be arraigned in the morning and likely out on bail by noon."

I shifted the suitcase to my other hand.

"Do you have a place to stay?" he asked.

"No. Not really."

"Hop in back," he offered, "There's a motel a mile along this road. If you like, I'll bring you there."

And he did. I woke the motel clerk, got a room and was back at Paul's address sitting on the porch steps the next day at noon. The house looked much more run down in the daylight.

Paul arrived an hour later and explained, "We were smoking weed on the beach when the cops showed up. So we ditched the stuff and figured, if we take our clothes off, they can't arrest us."

"Didn't work, huh?"

"No, not so well," was his reply.

We talked about what had happened in our lives the past three years. I was entering my junior year at MIT studying electrical engineering and Paul had two pending court cases and was a damn good surfer.

"If you're not working, how do you afford this place?" I inquired as I looked around.

"My dad sends me money."

"Where is he?"

"Your guess is as good as mine," he answered, "He was here last year for a while."

I hung around for a few tedious days including being woken up at 4:30 one morning to the cry, "SURF'S UP!"

We loaded old cars with gear, headed to another beach and after a few hours of trying to teach me to surf, we sat around while I was offered pills; "red ones for up and yellow for down, man... I think..."

An astounding number of his surfer friends asked me, "Is your hair really blonde? Like... you really don't bleach it, man?"

The last day I was there, Paul asked me to accompany him and his girlfriend, Monica, to Guadalajara, Mexico so she could find out about an abortion. It was my only visit south of the border.

When the subject of the money he owed me came up, I said, "Keep it. You need it more than I do."

I flew home the next day and I was like... *"really glad to get home... man."*

. . .

Fifteen years later I got a letter from him saying that he and Monica would be in Boston and could they come by and spend the night.

They arrived, we visited "Cheers" bar, talked about old times for a while then more current topics.

"We're not exactly married," he told us when Monica was in the restroom.

"No kids yet?" I asked.

"God no, she hates them," Paul said.

"We have three now," Donna responded pointedly.

The silence was followed by my saying, "Let's go back to my house for dessert."

Monica returned to the table, reached in her bag and spoke, "Hey, before we get to your house do you mind if I'm carrying?"

I thought maybe she was pregnant after all, but then she lifted a revolver half way out of her handbag with two fingers.

"I have a gun with me," she announced, "Is that okay?"

After an uncomfortable few seconds I said, "Oh... I'm not so sure... that it's a such good idea."

"No!" said Donna, "we have three small children. No!"

Yeah. That's what I meant, I said to myself

I don't remember the details but we skipped dessert, they stayed at the Holiday Inn down the street that night and then continued their trip the next day. I haven't seen either of them since.

Father Knows Best?

"You wait 'til your father gets home," my mother said, while putting a band-aid on her finger. She had cut it while tucking in the sheets on my bed and coming upon various clock parts I had hidden under the mattress. (The ones that wouldn't fit, after I took the clock apart and tried to get it back together.) It seemed like an ideal hiding place at the time to a five year old.

All too soon, Dad arrived home.

"Where's supper?" he said, "It's five o'clock."

"Wait until you hear what your son did today," she replied.

"Now what?" Dad said as he sat down at the table ready to eat.

Mom explained about the dismantled clock. Then to add insult to injury, she placed the remains of the timepiece, instead of his supper, in front of him. He inspected the mechanical carcass, then called me over.

"You couldn't get it back together, huh?" he asked.

"No," I squeaked while looking at the floor.

"After supper I'll show you how you should have done it. Now, go wash up," he ordered.

"Al, you can't--" my mother began.

"How's he going to learn if he can't take things apart," Dad interrupted, "Now, where's supper?"

. . .

When I was very young and there were people around, my Dad thought it was funny to answer "No," as I began to ask *any* question.

"Dad, can I--"

"NO!" he would say and all would laugh (except for me, of course.)

One day I hurried up the stairs and into the kitchen, ran up to my dad and said, "Hey Dad--"

And he immediately said, "NO!"

"But Dad--"

"NO!" he said again to laughter all around. (It's odd what grownups think is funny.)

I thought for a minute then looked at him and said, "It's not a question of yes or no. The trunk of the car is open."

I heard my Dad retell this story a hundred times. "Pretty good for a three year old kid," he would say. It's the only compliment he ever let me hear. I think it was his way of saying, "I love you."

. . .

One evening after supper, dad took me out to his new 1956 Chrysler Windsor, opened the trunk and showed me a sealed five gallon container of paint.

"Take this inside," he said, "and tomorrow paint the cellar floor."

I struggled to carry the bucket inside and the next day, starting over by the boiler, painted my way out of the cellar, back toward the stairs. The paint was battleship gray and printed on the can in large letters was: PROPERTY OF U.S. GOV'T.

This is so cool, I thought, *just like being in the navy.*

When dad came home that night he looked from the stairs and I could tell from the lack of any complaints that he was happy with the job.

"It'll be dry by morning," he said and then we went upstairs and had supper.

Next morning he checked it again.

"Because it's good paint it dries slow," he said, "It'll be dry by evening," then he went off to work.

That evening after looking at the cellar, dad decided to read the small print on the side of the can. Hidden amid many paragraphs we saw:

> This paint is formulated to have an extreme shelf life of twenty years. Drier <u>must</u> be added before use.

"What's drier?" I asked.

"I'll tell you tomorrow," he replied.

Beginning the following morning, I spent four days wiping the gray liquid off of the cellar floor with rags and balled up newspaper. I was originally told to use gasoline to help with the task but Uncle Billy who lived next door mentioned that if the boiler came on and ignited the gas vapors the house might end up on the Moon, so it was just me and newspaper. If I've ever had a worse job, I can't recall it. I have inherited many things from my dad, most are pretty good but there is one thing I wish I could change: I'd read directions *first*.

. . .

Then there was that perfect sunny and cool day late in the Autumn of 1958; we had already raked up a lot of leaves into a pile on the flagstone patio in our backyard so my father took the opportunity to cut and prune branches from the many trees around and added them to the heap.
Now what to do with all this, Dad must have said to himself.
He had an idea. He would burn it.
He lit match after match but couldn't get the pile to burn. He tried a small blowtorch and again failed to ignite the damp leaves. So he went to the shed where we kept the new gasoline powered lawnmower and came out with one of the red metal containers of fuel, poured some over the pile and threw a match.
WHOOOSH!
Flames shot into the air along with black smoke, a column of which rose a hundred feet into the sky before even beginning to disperse. My dad couldn't have been happier as he raked and shoveled the debris toward the inferno.
Unfortunately, the neighbors weren't so happy and they called the fire department, who arrived in moments and as the firemen were hosing down the conflagration the chief approached my dad.
"What happened here?" he asked.
"I don't know," Dad responded, "It was fine. I guess the wind came up."
"You're not supposed to have an un-contained fire in town. You know that, don't you."
"I had it contained until the wind--"
"In future, use a burn barrel or bag the leaves and the town will pick them up," he interrupted then abruptly walked to the truck which was now ready to leave.
The siren sounded briefly to alert the non-existent traffic on our quiet street and the truck was gone. Dad stood looking at the mess

that the backyard flagstone patio had become and began raking the blackened debris into a pile.

Now what to do with all this, Dad must have said to himself. He had an idea. He would burn it. But of course it was too wet now to burn easily so... he went to the shed and came out with another red metal container of fuel.

The firemen had, of course, just put out the fire but somewhere deep in that pile must have lurked an ember. No threat in a wet pile of leaves but when he poured the gasoline onto the mound--
WHOOOSH!

Flames shot into the air along with black smoke, a column of which rose a hundred feet into the sky before even beginning to disperse. The flame had also continued up the gasoline stream to the can, causing it to shoot into the air, landing twenty feet away and adding to the blaze. The entire yard was afire.

Fortunately, the neighbors (having become quite vigilant, living next to my dad) called the fire department. The same truck, which had not yet returned to the station had to turn around and was back in front of our house. The firemen quickly extinguished the fire (again) as the chief warily approached my dad.

"What the hell is going on here?" he asked but didn't wait for an answer, "Are you crazy?"

Now, the chief waited for an answer.

"I was just cleaning up the mess and it--"

The chief's face reddened, he stomped his foot down and in a loud voice said, "If you ever--" then thought better of whatever he was going to say. He began again more calmly, "The Public Works Department will send a truck tomorrow morning, to clean this up. Don't rake it. Don't sweep it. Don't *touch* it. Do you understand?"

A little smile came to dad's face, "That's a good idea," he said.

The truck drove off once more.

Dad stood looking at the now incredible, wet, blackened mess that was our backyard.

I have no idea what he was thinking at that moment but after a minute he went inside the house, sat in his favorite reclining chair and began reading Time magazine.

It was the first time I had witnessed my dad giving up on a harebrained idea and I know the whole neighborhood was fortunate that he did; but still, it was a bittersweet moment. Up until that time he and I both believed he could do anything.

Now, we weren't quite so sure.

...

I came home over Christmas break my freshman year in college to find my dad in the cellar wiring a timer for the outside lights.

"Hi Dad, How's it going?" I said.

"Hi," he said and continued working.

I watched him for a minute then said, "You're wiring that wrong--"

He put his hands by his side, stood to his full five foot, five inch height, looked at me and said, "This isn't my first time you know. I've done this before." I had clearly tapped into some pent up energy. "You go off to school and think you know everything about everything. Well... maybe you haven't... "

He continued speaking but whatever else he was saying was unintelligible and he was back to wiring the timer (still incorrectly).

"Dad, I am studying electrical engineering. And I can see that you're wiring it wrong. It will be a short--"

He stopped and looked at me.

"You're just like your mother," he said then took a step back, admiring his work, "There! It's ready to go."

He flipped on the breaker and began to advance the clock to the current time.

"Dad," I said, "It's going to--"

KA- BOOM

Smoke filled the small (now darker) space and little bits of hot copper flew everywhere. Slowly the smoke subsided and my dad was again visible a few steps back from where he had been.

"You all right?" I asked.

There was a long silence then his eyes met mine and he said, "Okay. If you're so smart; you wire it!" then he walked past me, handing me the tools and went upstairs.

I bought a new timer and installed it the next day. It turned out to be a watershed moment in our lives. After that, I noticed that he actually asked my advise *before* beginning a project and I'm sure that was not easy for him. Or for me.

. . .

"Dad, I think it's too big to get out by hand. Maybe we should just cut it down and grind the stump," I suggested.

"What are you talking about," he replied.

Here we go, I thought.

Dad opened the trunk of his new 1961 Olds Cutlass, leaned in and came up with a hank of nylon rope he had likely "borrowed" from the Air Force.

"Here. Tie this onto the trunk of the tree," he ordered as he handed me one end of the coil.

He walked over to a telephone pole a few feet away on the sidewalk in front of our house where he attached a one foot piece of pipe on the other end of the rope for weight and on the third try, threw it over the cross-arm of the pole. Then he pulled the car out of the driveway and left the engine running.

"Pull that rope taut and tie it onto the bumper," he ordered.

This definitely isn't going to end well, I thought.

"What if it breaks?" I asked as he climbed in the car.

"Don't worry; it won't break. You're just like your mother," he said.

He shifted into low and very slowly drove up the street while watching the tree in the rear-view mirror. 10 feet-- Nothing happened. 20 feet-- Still nothing happened. 30 feet-- No noticeable movement but the once half inch nylon rope was stretched so tightly it was only a quarter inch wide. I couldn't take my eyes off of the twelve foot pine tree. 31 feet. 32 feet. 33-- BOING !

The tree was gone! One second it was there, as it had been since I was 4 years old, and the next it was replaced with a three foot deep hole in the ground. Dad had also seen the tree disappear in the rear view mirror. He looked over at me. I shrugged my shoulders, then heard a whoosh as the tree began it's decent. Dirt came raining down. The tree had catapulted into the air and came down across the street in Mr. and Mrs. Callahan's front yard-- rope still attached-- with such force that it penetrated two feet into their lawn.

I was afraid to move but looked up to see if anything else might be coming down from the sky as Dad got out of the car.

"Don't just stand there," he said, "Help me get the tree."

"Good thing they're not home, huh?" I said suppressing a giggle.

"You think they'll notice this hole in their lawn?"

"Help me drag this behind our house then get a rake and straighten up this mess," he said.

I never heard another word about the incident. I don't know if the Callahans assumed that a meteorite had landed in their front yard or what.

What I've figured out from observing all this, is that despite all the good things that I've learned from my father, I really am just like my mother.

Dad, Mom and me in 1949

Hey, Baby

In June 1962, to celebrate the end of the school year, Maryanne Ferrara had a party in her backyard on Herman Street. She strung lights, filled coolers with ice, and for music, I brought the reel to reel tape recorder that my Uncle Sal had just given me for graduation, along with an impressive collection of oldies that I had been taping off the radio for years. Unfortunately, a lot of them had bits of Arnie (Woo-Woo) Ginsberg's voice leading in or out of the songs, but no one seemed to care.

It was a warm evening and almost everyone was there, even Tami Lydon who I had been dating up until a couple of months ago. Now, she wouldn't even acknowledge my presence. I knew why, but still found it hard to believe how rapidly and totally her feelings could change. The things I didn't understand about girls could have filled a book then. (Not much has changed.)

Early in the evening as she walked by, I said, "Hi. How have you been?"

Her reply was a brief stare.

Hmm, seems to be cooling off a bit, I said under my breath.

She was there with her new boyfriend, Bobby VanAllen. He was a starting guard on the Winthrop high school championship basketball team but I hardly knew him (which was fine with me.)

If she wants him, she can have him, was my attitude.

Maryanne's parents were keeping an eye on things from inside the house. They could be seen peering through the curtains from time to time, so a few of the boys went off to drink beer behind the junior high school down the street. They were led by Richie Stark, who as well as being a sports jock was liked by everyone. He was a tall, athletic football player type, who could (and did) pass for twenty-one in out-of-town liquor stores.

The 1955 Ford that my brother-in-law had loaned me was parked out front and I had hopes of driving Lynn Stiller home-- if she ever showed up. We had been dating for a couple of months (and was the reason Tami wasn't speaking to me.)

The boys were returning from drinking down the street and the party was getting a little noisy.

"Turn up the music," Maryanne said, "and get out there and dance!"

I turned up the volume and looked around but saw no sign of Lynn. Then someone unplugged one of the strings of lights. The parents peered out the window nervously.

I checked the playlist, saw that a slow song was coming up next and looked around for someone to ask to dance.

POP! POP! POP!

"What was that?" a girl near me cried out. The dancing stopped while the music (*Hey, Baby* by Bruce Channel) kept blaring.

POP! POP!

Now the crowd was scattering. Everyone seemed to be running from the direction of the driveway into the neighboring yards. Everyone except Bobby VanAllen. He was on the ground, motionless, ten feet from me.

"What the hell is going on?" I shouted.

Then I spotted a man standing erect, yelling incoherently and slowly walking down the driveway. He had something in his hand.

"A gun!" someone shouted.

I think I cried out, "Get down, Get down!" and ducked behind a large red metal cooler with *drink Coca-Cola* written on the side.

The man took another step. *Hey, Baby* played on.

POP! POP! click. click.

I was frozen, still trying to make sense of what was happening when I saw Richie Stark running *toward* the man.

click. click.

Suddenly, the man turned and ran up the driveway, across a small lawn and as he reached his porch, Richie tackled him. A few more boys helped hold the man down until the police arrived.

When I could stand up, I turned off the tape recorder.

An ambulance came and took Bobby away on a stretcher. The girls were crying and attempting to calm Tami who was shrieking uncontrollably. The boys gathered round Richie and tried to figure out how he could have been so heroic.

"You think it was it the beer?" we wondered aloud.

The police found more loaded guns in the man's living room so we soon realized that Richie may well have saved all our lives. The next time I heard of him he was a policeman (honest) in the town. I can't help thinking, that incident totally shaped his future. Unfortunately it shaped Bobby's future as well. The bullet had hit his spine and he was paralyzed from the waist down.

Lynn never showed up that night so I gathered up my tapes and audio equipment and drove home alone.

A week later I saw Tami. We talked for a few minutes.

"I'm really sorry about Bobby," I said, "How's he doing?"

"Better. He may not walk for a long time, but they say he will."

"That's good news."

The mood shifted and she said, "I'm sorry for the way I've acted toward you lately."

Trying to be gracious I said, "No, I deserved it."

"Yes you did," she said, and walked away.

Uncle Sal

I took the Green line from Auditorium to Government Center then the Blue line to Orient Heights and finally a bus to Main Street Winthrop; eventually arriving home on a Sunday evening in the late fall of 1963 to find my Dad sitting at the kitchen table sharing coffee, biscotti and some gossip with my uncle Salvatore, who everyone called Sal.

My father gave me the cursory acknowledgment you'd expect from someone who knew that you'd only come home from college to ask for something; while Uncle Sal, on the other hand, greeted me more enthusiastically.

"Hello Ernest. Always good to see you," he announced.

It's clear to me now that Sal was my favorite (and certainly my most interesting) uncle; but I didn't really think much about that then. I sat down at the table and hoped he would leave soon so I could talk to my father alone. But when the conversation turned to *what crooks bankers were*, I knew I would never outlast them.

So I took a deep breath and interrupted, "Dad, I think I'd like to get another car."

My first car had been a used, 1959, white Triumph Herald Coupe. It had a little 900 cc engine, cost $600 and was certainly no match for a black 1956 Buick in a head on collision! Fortunately, I was only slightly hurt in the accident and was recently awarded $2200 in the resulting lawsuit (plus legal costs) but alas, the coupe was totaled. My Dad had bought it for me my first year at MIT but now, as a subway riding sophomore, I had my eye (and heart set) on a new 1964 Triumph Roadster. I lived at college but never having bought a car myself, I was more than willing to visit home for some advice (and the additional $1000 I would need.)

"I'm thinking of getting another Triumph. Like the Herald... but a TR-4. You know, a sports car. Brand new. Blue..." I stumbled along, not being sure when to quit.

My dad looked at me with the little smile that often accompanied his attempts at humor, and said, "Go ahead; I won't stop you."

He glanced over at Sal expecting some support but uncle was busy dunking a rock hard biscuit in his coffee.

At least he didn't say no, I thought as I continued my appeal, "Well that's the thing... I'll need a little more money and--"

"How much?" he asked but didn't wait for an answer, "and where are you getting it?"

I-- perhaps somewhat wishfully-- thought he meant, where was I getting *the car...* and since I had an answer to *that* question I replied, "Well they're hard to find but there's a dealer in Boston on Commonwealth Ave. that I think--"

My father sighed and put his hands on the table (never a good sign) and began, "Listen..."

This was not going the way I hoped. He was definitely getting aggravated.

I knew I should have waited, I thought as my face reddened.

Abruptly, Uncle Sal put down his half eaten biscuit, looked at my father, then at me and cleared his throat.

"ERNEST," he said loudly enough to stop Dad from talking, "HERE'S what I want you to do."

I was all ears. As far as I was concerned, anything would be better than what my dad would be saying.

"You have some time tomorrow?" Uncle asked, back in his normal voice.

I nodded.

"You know where Seymour Chevrolet is in Cambridge?"

I nodded.

"You go to Seymour Chevrolet and ask for Dick..." Uncle Sal lightly bit on his thumb for a second then went on, "Tell him... (*a pause while he bit some more*)... tell him Louie from National Auto Sales sent you."

I must have made a face indicating slight confusion.

"He'll know what it means," he said. "You tell him what it is you want. He'll take care of you."

"Do they sell Triumphs?" I asked.

"Ernest," He answered with a touch of impatience in his voice, "just tell him Louie from--"

"National Auto Sales sent me," I said, "I know. Okay."

. . .

Let me tell you a little about my uncle. He was short, bald and though related to us only through marriage (his last name was Donato), could be and was easily mistaken for Dad. In fact, from a distance they were indistinguishable. The similarity ended there though. My Dad was a really good mechanic and taught me all about tools and how to use them. He could fix anything but he never took the easy way. Everything he did, ultimately became remarkably complicated but he never gave up and seemed to enjoy it all the more. He always got the job done; at least it seemed that way to a young me.

On the other hand, Uncle Sal was laid back, always looking for the easy way and usually managed to get others to do things for him. He knew how the world worked and his explanations made things seem simple. Even at a young age I noticed that he was invariably right when he would explain the story behind a headline (especially if a crime was involved). Months later, when the truth would be revealed to all, I'd recall that Uncle had nailed it.

Also, he was remarkably good at predicting when his race horse was going to win at the local track. He owned the horse with a friend, who Uncle referred to as his *associate*, named Rocky Palmari

Rita-Louise (named after their wives), ran only at the tracks nearby and Uncle usually warned my Dad not to bother betting on her.

Except once in a while, Sal would call, announcing, "Today might be a good day to wager some money at the track," and hang up.

My Dad, due to his confusion around the meaning of win, place and show, often didn't profit from the tip but on the days that Uncle Sal called, Rita-Louise always seemed a little more motivated than usual.

· · ·

Every few weeks, Uncle and Rocky would come to our house for supper. They were always accompanied by another associate (His name was Tony) who would stand out front, immobile, arms crossed, while chewing bubble gum and watch the cars go by as we ate inside. I never saw Tony when he wasn't working on one of the large gumballs (called Jawbreakers) that he always had in his pockets. The bulge in his sport-coat clearly showed just how many he must be carrying.

At the dining room table, my mother would say, "Sal, tell your friend to come in and have a dish of pasta."

And Sal would say, "I don't pay him to eat."

• • •

When I was 11, dad got a phone call late one Friday night. From my room I could hear Mom and Dad arguing as he got dressed; then he went out. In the morning, they still were going at it but now there was a small, gray, locked metal box on the side table in the dining room. I could tell Mom didn't want it in the house. Uncle Sal had apparently used his one phone call to alert Dad to get the box before the police did. When no one was looking, I picked it up (it was surprisingly light) and shook it, but its contents remained a mystery. After a few days, Uncle and Rocky came by, had a dish of pasta (while Tony waited outside, blowing bubbles) then carried the box away. Rumors flew everywhere in the family but all I ever figured out was that it had to do with insurance and uncle's 32 foot cabin cruiser that mysteriously burned to its waterline last fall.

This was all especially exciting because a few months before, I had been on *that* boat, alone in Boston Harbor with Uncle Sal, and... he had let me steer it! He was standing near me as we moved along at a good clip, water spraying up onto the windshield, when I turned the wheel way too sharply. He fell against the rail and tumbled overboard! I looked back and watched him frantically yelling something as the distance between us increased! I couldn't hear anything above the engine noise and all I could think to do was turn the key; shutting off the engine. I had heard that he had been in the Navy during the war so I thought nothing of how quickly he swam (though fully clothed) the fifty yards back to the boat. I remained seated and quiet, expecting the worst, as he slowly climbed back on board.

"Sorry," I said meekly.

Standing soaking wet, catching his breath, he looked at me, rubbed his hands back over his head as if he had hair to slick back and calmly declared, "Ernest... that was quick thinking."

He went below then re-emerged in his bathing suit and said, "Let's get this thing started so you can take us home."

The trip back to the dock involved low speed and very gradual turns. He never mentioned the incident to me again.

...

During my high school years, Uncle would call and ask if my friends and I would like to make a little money.

"Bring your friends and meet us Friday night..." he would say, "...at the Odd Fellows Hall parking lot ," or, "...at the Knights of Columbus parking lot" or some other similar location in town-- never the same place twice.

A tractor trailer truck would show up and items would be auctioned right out the back of the trailer. My friends and I were the "runners"; bringing the items to the highest bidder and collecting the money. It wasn't hard work, we made some cash and had some fun. In fact, everyone seemed to enjoy themselves. Even my Uncle and his friends (associates?) often seemed surprised and pleased with the items that were brought out onto the tailgate to be sold.

Occasionally there would be other jobs where my friends and I would make some cash; like the time Uncle needed a truckload of heavy milling machines moved into an empty store on Bennington Street. My friends and I (with associate Tony's help) spent hours wheeling the machines carefully down a ramp from the truck, across the sidewalk and into a large storefront.

After the eighth one, I looked around, then went to Uncle and said, "You know Uncle Sal, there isn't enough electricity coming into this building to run half these lathes."

Tony, standing nearby, popped a bubble and said "He's a regular Einstein, ain't he?"

Uncle Sal shot a look at him that would have killed a smaller man and then turned to me and said quietly, "It don't matter if you and I know they can't run... as long as *everyone* don't know that."

"Oh," I said as if I understood what he was talking about. (Grasping the concept of "laundering" money was still years in my future.)

...

Sal and Rocky were partners in a Chinese Restaurant in East Boston that was rumored to stay open after hours and condone gambling on the premises. But to be fair, I was only there during normal hours, usually eating one of their signature dishes (Lobster Palmeri or Shrimp Donato) and never saw any sign of illegal activities.

...

When I graduated high school, Uncle Sal came by my house one night to see me. This was notable for two reasons: he had never come by my house *solely* to see me *and* he was bearing a gift.

He placed a Wollensak reel to reel tape recorder on my desk and said, "Ernest, your dad tells me you've decided to go to MIT in the fall. Wise choice."

"This is amazing. I've always wanted one," I said, "It must have cost a fortune."

"I thought you might like it," he said without much emotion. Then after looking around my room, he leaned toward me and said in almost a whisper, "By the way, there's no need to tell anyone where you got it."

"Oh," I said, "Uh... sure."

...

Every year at M.I.T., there was a freshman - sophomore rivalry called Field Day, where each class competed in sporting events on a Saturday morning in the fall. Tradition held that each class tried to kidnap the officers of the other class, keeping them from the festivities. The night before Field Day 1962, a few of us (freshmen) captured the sophomore vice-president (or maybe he was the treasurer), tied him up and brought him to a prearranged hideaway. I had originally thought we might hold him at my house but the week before, my father suggested that Sal might have some better ideas. He did.

When I told Uncle of our plan he smiled and said, "I have just the place Ernest. A vacant storefront in Orient Heights I just picked up." He told me the address, handed me a key and said, "If you can have some fun with it, so be it."

With considerable effort we got our duct-taped prisoner safely inside the former barbershop and handcuffed him to a pipe column away from the front windows. He made quite a ruckus, which was made all the louder by the stark surroundings. This is when I learned that unless you're willing to kill someone; you can't make them be quiet. And he definitely would not be quiet!

About 2:30 AM, a rotating blue light appeared out front. We could see a flashlight beam darting around, followed by a tap at the glass front door.

Since this had been my bright idea, I was pushed forward to unlock the door and was greeted with, "What's going on in here?"

A uniformed officer of the law turned the flashlight, shining it on our captive, handcuffed to a post and trying to speak despite being gagged with a handkerchief.

"Geth mee outh ov herrgh!"

"Well, officer," I began, trying to stay calm and still be heard above the din, "actually..."

Oh my god, I thought, *there was no way we aren't in serious trouble.*

"...actually," I continued, "this is just a college prank and my Uncle Sal Donato said we could use this..."

"Sal Donato?" the policeman interrupted, "Sal is your uncle?"

I nodded, "Yes," having no idea where this was going.

The policeman lowered his flashlight, stood a little straighter and said, "How is Sal?"

Everyone-- sophomore and freshmen alike-- was stunned. It got eerily quiet.

He continued, "Tell him I said hello... but could you keep it down a bit? The sound carries something awful at this hour."

"Certainly," I said, after I had regained the ability to speak.

The policeman turned and left.

"Wow!" said the other freshmen.

"Wath tha Fugft?" said the sophomore.

...

I spotted the sign, SEE THE U.S.A. IN YOUR SEYMOUR CHEVERLET, from two blocks away as I hurried along Mass Ave after my Monday morning calculus class. It was just noon as I arrived at the showroom full of shiny 1964 Chevy Bel Airs,

Impalas, Corvairs and a bright yellow Malibu convertible. There wasn't a soul in sight. So I walked to the back and there in a cubicle I saw a middle-aged man quietly sitting at a desk. He was wearing a Madras sport-coat and had his back toward me. On the desk in front of him was a partially eaten sandwich (tuna, I think) on a sheet of wrinkled wax paper. The man was leaning forward, holding a small carton of milk with a bent straw up to his lips.

I stood in the doorway and cleared my throat.

He spun in his chair when he heard me and looked up.

"Mmmf?" he said into the straw.

"I'm looking for Dick," I said with my most adult voice.

"Can't you see that I'm eating?" he said after composing himself.

He was clearly annoyed at the young, likely penniless college student (holding a calculus book, no less) standing at his door.

I backed into the hall, walked away toward the showroom then very slowly made my way back to his door. He took a bite from the sandwich just as he noticed me again.

"What is it you want?" he said after swallowing.

"Are you Dick?" I asked.

"Yes. I'm Dick," he replied impatiently.

Here goes nothing, I thought.

Then I said, "Louie from National Auto Sales sent me and--"

Instantly there was a pronounced change of the atmosphere in the room. Dick sat up straight in his chair and with a remarkably well choreographed series of moves, slid open the top drawer of his desk with one hand, while with the other, swept the wax paper (containing the remaining portion of the sandwich) and the milk carton off the desktop and into the open drawer.

He then quickly closed the drawer, turned in his chair to face me, pointed to a seat at the side of the desk and said, "Sit. What can I do for you?"

So I sat and explained at some length about the Triumph TR4 roadster that I was looking for. One with the optional wire wheels with knock off hubs, independent rear suspension, dual carburetors, leather covered steering wheel, real wood dash, AM-FM radio and black snap-on tonneau cover. And of course, it had to be Blue.

I added apologetically, "And I know the extras will take some--"

He was no longer listening to me; but instead had a phone

propped against this ear while whispering into the mouthpiece and scribbling on a yellow pad. When he finally hung up, he wrote something on a small note sheet, folded it in half and slid it to me.

"Please, please let it be less than $3200," I prayed silently as I unfolded the paper.

It read... $ 2200.

I was stunned and uncertain how to proceed. "Does this--"

"Loaded. Everything you wanted," he assured, "When would you like it? Would tomorrow be okay?"

"Tomorrow?" I repeated, wishing I hadn't made it a question. "Tomorrow... yes, tomorrow would be fine," I re-stated in my most adult voice.

"Good then," said Dick, "And you be sure and tell Louie I took care of you."

I nodded as I got up, peeking again at the number on the slip of paper. It still read $2200.

"Should I pay--"

"Tomorrow. A check. Does that work?"

"A personal check?" I asked incredulously, forgetting to use my most adult voice.

"Sure, why not?" he said.

I shrugged.

"Fine," said Dick, standing now with hand extended. "Then I'll see you tomorrow at two."

Donna & Snoopy in TR-4 (1965)

We shook hands then I walked through the showroom and out into the sun. I was so excited I began talking to myself as I walked back up Mass Ave.

"Yes! Yes! Yes!" I shouted under my breath, "Tomorrow! Yes!"

I stopped, took a deep breath and looked back toward the showroom. I wondered if Dick had retrieved the tuna sandwich. I wondered if the milk carton had landed upright in the drawer. I wondered, *Who... the... hell... is... Louie?*

With no additional money needed from my Dad, I picked up the car the next day and it was the best (and most fun) car I have ever owned. Mechanically it sucked (it was made in England after all) but in 1963 you couldn't get any "cooler" than a two seat British sports car.

...

I didn't see Uncle Sal much for a couple of years after that, both of us moving on our separate tracks. I heard about him from my Dad and saw him briefly at the occasional holiday dinner but that was about it. Until in the early spring of 1966, as my college graduation neared, Uncle appeared during one of my increasingly rare visits home. It was a warm evening and he found me alone outside.

"Hello Ernest. Always good to see you."

He moved a little closer and put has hand on my arm.

"We need to talk," he said, "Do you mind if I give you some advice?"

"No," I said.

Now what, I thought.

He began, "If life offers you something, you gotta grab it!" His grip on my arm increased, "Have you ever heard that?"

I shrugged my shoulders, "I guess."

He went on, "When I was a young fellow, during the depression, I took any odd job I could find. I went house to house and offered to clean people's cars for a nickel... then I'd steal whatever I could find from the glove box or the trunk and move on. I managed to get by that way. They were tough times. You following me?"

"Sort of..."

He forged ahead despite my uncertainty, "But then World War Two came along and I joined the Navy. I took what I could, put it aside and after the War, opened surplus stores and made some good money, met the right people; moved up. You see?" He put his arm around my shoulders so he could speak into my ear, "The war was an opportunity. Sure, it was bad... but it was good. You see that?" he said softly.

"I... I guess so."

He apparently took my reply as a definite yes.

Still speaking quietly he said, "I've done pretty well you know, but... I don't... have a son..."

During the pause that followed I was careful not to mention his daughter, my cousin Sally.

Now he spoke a little louder, "But I watched you grow up..." he went on very deliberately, "and I find out things... I know things... and you seem like a real bright kid... so... I want you to know... there's a job waiting for you if you want it."

This was so out of the blue that I didn't know what to say.

So I said, "I think I'm going to be a teacher. You know... high school... math maybe."

He slowly took his arm away and straightened his sport jacket. He thought for a long moment.

"Teacher?" he said with an inflection I had never heard used with that word before. "Well Ernest," he paused a few seconds, "if you want... to throw your life away... you go ahead." He didn't sound angry; perhaps just a little disappointed. He slowly walked back toward the house, and without turning around said, "The job will be here if you want it."

I stood perfectly still for a while.

Job? I thought. *He doesn't even <u>have</u> a real job. What job could he possibly be talking about? Would I replace Tony?*

I left that night without finding out any more about it.

• • •

I didn't see him again until a few months later at my wedding. He and Aunt Rita presented Donna and I with two dozen gold encrusted wine goblets as a gift. They didn't mention if I should tell anyone where we got them (or why we might need twenty-four of them.)

I didn't doubt that I had made the right decision, ignoring the job offer, but I was still curious about what exactly it was. When things calmed down at the reception, I thought about asking but never got up the nerve.

...

When I bought my Yamaha motorcycle in 1967, Massachusetts had started requiring a driving test for the special license. It was no problem and I mentioned to my dad at a Sunday lunch that I had an appointment at the Nashua Street registry at noon the next day. When I arrived, after driving over from my Commonwealth Avenue apartment, there was Uncle Sal, standing at the registry entrance with a uniformed state trooper. I parked the bike then walked up the steps.

"Hey Uncle, what are you doing here? I have a driving test--"

"I know, Ernest," he said, "Good to see you." Then he turned to the trooper and said, "This is the nephew I was telling you about. He handles a motorcycle like he was born on it."

The policeman wrote something on a pad, tore off a sheet, handed it to me and said, "Here. I'm pretty busy so give this to the clerk inside. You're all set."

After having practiced figure-eights all week I was momentarily speechless, but then managed to say, "Thank you."

"Ernest, you take me for a ride someday," Uncle Sal said with a big smile as I went into the registry. He and the state trooper continued talking outside.

...

The last time I saw my uncle, he was sitting with his daughter, Sally, in a restaurant.

"He's a week short of his 95th birthday," she said.

"Hi uncle Sal, happy birthday," I said loud enough that he would likely hear me.

He looked up from his meal but displayed no emotion.

Sally said something in his ear, then his face brightened a bit and he replied, "Hello Ernest, always good to see you."

"You too Uncle; you too," I said.

His attention returned to his plate.

Wow, a lot of years have passed, I thought.

It was clearly too late now to ask:

- how did he know when Rita-Louise was going to win...
- or where did those tractor trailers came from...
- or what was in that gray metal box...
- or who burned the boat...

-or could he *possibly* have had anything to do with my getting into MIT...

-or if the exactly $2200 price at Seymour Chevrolet was just a coincidence...

-or was that state trooper really too busy to give me the driving test...

-or what that job he offered me would have been...

-and not least... *who the hell was Louie?*

But now that I think of it, it's just as well I never asked... some questions are best left unanswered.

Snoopy on Triumph Herald after head-on collision (1963)

SAE

After the freshmen orientation lecture, I walked out of Kresge Auditorium, stood amid nine hundred teenage boys (and ten girls), looked across the street at MIT's main entrance with it's huge columns and said to myself, *What in the world am I doing here?*

I was surrounded by the smartest eighteen year-old's in the country (maybe the world) and couldn't have felt more out of place if I had been brought to this distant planet by an alien spaceship. I was thrilled-- and terrified-- that this was happening to me and up until now my over-developed sense of self-assurance had helped me cope, but suddenly, I was here... the moment had arrived... and I felt overwhelmed. I suspect that most everyone that night had those feelings; but we all dealt with them in different ways. Some with unchecked exuberance, others feigned indifference and some simply remained quiet. I didn't know a soul. It felt like I was about to try to cross a vast ocean all by myself. I stood silently.

"You're Ernie... right?" said a familiar voice, "Bill Morton here. Remember me?"

I did remember... and shook his outstretched hand.

The previous July I had received a phone call that began, "Hi, I'm a student at MIT... and I'd like to come and speak with you and your parents, if you'll let me, about where you'll be living in September. My name is Bill Morton"

I knew that I wanted to live on campus and expected I'd be told where by the school; but Bill came, sat at the kitchen table and explained about fraternities, rush week, dormitories and the like.

It all sounded great but I didn't *really* know quite what to expect.

Now he and a few of his fraternity brothers were standing in front of me carrying makeshift Greek-lettered 'SAE' signs.

"Why don't you come and stay at our house tonight," he said, "and tomorrow we'll show you around."

As if a fog was lifted, I now saw that there were a sea of perhaps a hundred signs, representing the 30 or 40 living groups on campus, all bobbing up and down surrounding the auditorium. We made our way through the dense crowd to a waiting car that took us across the Harvard Bridge to Beacon Street.

If I was indeed about to cross an ocean, then that night, Sigma Alpha Epsilon fraternity at least offered me a life-jacket. But that was on Friday night and classes began next week. I had a lot to learn. My life-path was about to take a sharp turn and except for my girlfriend and my underwear, everything was totally new to me. The fraternity owned two houses, 480 and 484 Beacon Street, with 36 brothers and 16 pledges living there when classes started. MIT was a pretty competitive place, so getting the sixteen pledges to be "brothers" was not easy. Taking a cue from the military I suppose, we were made to depend on each other and over time, grew close. I had classes six days a week (including a 3 hour chemistry lab on Saturday morning!) and work to perform at the house and homework to do (a lot of homework) but somehow it all got done and after three or four weeks, I figured out how to squeeze in a few minutes of fun as well. Pledges had phone duty and wake-up duty and a ritual at the dinner table of being called on to stand and recite the biographical information of all the brothers at the meal. I still remember a few; such as: Fredrick Samuel Souk, class of 1965, from Alexandria, Virginia, in course 14, Political Science.

We had a cook (Mrs. Miller) and a butler (Joseph Franklin) who had been employed by SAE for twenty-four years when I arrived! They were our parents, confessors, servers, consciences and weather forecasters. They connected a bunch of over-achieving, privileged kids to the real world. If you were ashamed to do something in front of them, you knew you shouldn't be doing it. They kept us grounded and were the face of the fraternity.

The first words spoken by alumni that visited the house were always, "How are Mrs. Miller and Joseph doing? Are they still here?"

Each fall, my fraternity threw one of the most anticipated parties of the year on campus. It was a classic toga party called *SAElor dance*. It took us weeks to prepare and a week to clean up and was probably the thing the neighbors liked the least about us. Although it was the sixties, the drug culture hadn't made it in a big way to our campus yet, so we were spared that temptation.

I picked Donna up most weekends and we spent Friday evening

to Sunday afternoon together. (I think we might have given her mother the impression that we had a live-in 'house mother.') Donna spent more time at SAE than anyone who wasn't a brother (except for Mrs. Miller and Joseph) and became part of the experience. When we broke up during my senior year, I wasn't the only one despondent.

"What were you thinking?" I was asked more than once.

"I wasn't thinking anything-- " I replied, but before I could add, "--s*he* dumped *me,*" they said, "Well, that's obvious!"

As an off campus living group, the fraternity was pretty much left to take care of itself and except for the time when a couple of the seniors brought a porn film back to the house and ran afoul of the FBI or the time during a snow storm that a brother lofted an "ice snowball" from the roof and it went clean through the windshield of the South Korean Ambassador's limousine on Beacon Street, we had little to do with any authority.

Each new term, every brother would bid for the room he wanted; decided by seniority, so there was a lot of moving around. I had a series of interesting roommates including Clarence Hunsucker III, who had gone to an exclusive private school with only eleven boys enrolled, so every student was required to be on the football team! Clancy was short and pudgy, with red hair and I can't recall ever seeing him out of his ROTC uniform. His father owned a vineyard in California where Caesar Chavez and the grape picker's union were striking at the time and we had some very heated discussions about whether or not a person deserved more than fifty cents an hour to pick grapes.

Bill Morton was assigned as my "Big Brother" when I was a pledge. He was a good guy and helped me tremendously. Also, as far as I could tell, he could drink more beer than any other human being. He should have graduated in 1965 but being in the naval reserve was called up during the 1963 Cuban missile crisis, then (inexplicably) stationed in Antarctica (during their winter) for six months! He ended up getting a chemistry degree at Northeastern University.

John Bueler was the biggest member of the fraternity and a star on our house inter-mural football team. Despite his size he was constantly apologizing for one thing or another.

"Oops, "he would say, "I didn't see you there. Sorry," as he brushed you back against the wall.

He avoided the draft (and the Vietnam War) when he was classified 4-F because his feet were too big!

Hank Perry was a born southern politician. He helped negotiate for days between the Social Security System and the Defense Department to get Joseph his rightful benefits even when it seemed the bureaucracy would win. He never did appear to be the 'engineer' type and in fact went on to be a congressman from Illinois.

Marlon Whiteman was on the wrestling team, ate raw meat, could lose five pounds (to fight in a lower weight class) faster than anyone I ever heard of and every night did five hundred sit ups (counting out every one) while I sat at my desk, eating a Hostess cupcake and trying to concentrate on a physics problem set.

Five hundred sit ups! And I don't think he ever lost a match!

Then there was Mike Newhouse.

He was the first member of my pledge class that I met on arriving and when I asked his name he said, "Humans can't pronounce it; so I go by Mike."

"Where are you from?" I asked.

"Everywhere," he replied, "My dad's a Colonel in the Army." After a pause he said, "I went to high school in the Azores."

"Do you have any brothers or sisters?"

"I don't know. My dad won't tell me," he answered and poured himself another Coke.

That entire term, I never once saw him study or turn down a chance to screw off. He was certainly fun to be with and it seemed he was always around when I would take a break from studying. Late one night, we snuck into the kitchen to make tapioca pudding. Mrs. Miller had to prepare recipes for fifty, so everything on the shelves was in very large packages. I poured some milk into a big pot and Mike brought over the huge box of tapioca.

"It says two tablespoons to a cup of milk," I mentioned.

"I've done this a hundred times," he boasted, "and that's nowhere near enough."

    He poured some from the box until he said, "That looks like enough."

We turned up the gas and began stirring. In a few minutes, mixing got difficult and required two hands. Soon Mike had to hold the pot while I struggled to stir the concoction until finally; the pot, the tapioca and the large spoon were one.

The next day Joseph retrieved the disaster from the dumpster and amazingly, he and Mrs. Miller managed to salvage the cooking utensils. I tried to appear surprised and sympathetic as she told me the story.

"Who would do such a thing?" she asked.

I shrugged.

Sadly (but predictably), Mike didn't return to MIT the next term and I never saw him again. I really missed him and his sense of humor. The last I heard, in the 1970's, he was a DJ at a Cleveland, Ohio radio station.

I lived at the fraternity house, including summers, until June, 1966 when I got married.

I was lucky I found Sigma Alpha Epsilon fraternity (or did it find me?) and although I was the house manager and then the treasurer, I could never repay the debt I owe it. Fraternities no longer enjoy the status that they once held but for me it was the right place at the right time and looking back, I'm not sure I would have survived without it. SAE was my home and (perhaps a bit dis-functional) family for my four years at college. I literally grew up there.

It was my lifeboat.

Road Trip

"Hop on," I shouted to Donna over the noise of the engine, "I might as well learn how to ride this thing with you on the back."

Donna donned her helmet, climbed onto the back of the used motorcycle we had just bought and put her arms around my waist.

"Hold on tight," I called out, "Here we go!"

We drove around the parking lot a few times while the man who had just sold us the bike, stood smoking a cigarette and trying to figure out what we were up to. He soon gave up and went inside. He had no way of knowing that I had never been on a motorcycle before. I had an AAA international driver's license with a checkmark next to *motorcycle,* only because no special license was needed to drive one in Massachusetts in 1966. Soon we were driving through the streets alongside the canals of Amsterdam, on our way back to the youth hostel where we were staying.

A few days before, we had begun our honeymoon in London after a flight from New York. We took a ferry across the North Sea to the Hague in Holland then hitch-hiked into the center. The following day we thumbed another ride into Amsterdam. The man who picked us up wanted to show us his mother's cottage with its flowers, so we stopped along the way in a tiny village and had tea and biscuits with her before being dropped off in the city.

The next day we found a bike shop and bought an Austrian made, 1961 Puch motorcycle. I had a chance to get a 1956 direct drive BMW, but I assumed that the newer bike would likely be less trouble. Events would prove my assumption wrong.

I needed insurance but after many phone calls, could only find one agent in far away Rotterdam who would sell insurance to an American Student.

"But I'm in Amsterdam," I said to the agent.

"Just drive here on the motorcycle," he replied, "it's only an hour and if anything happens I'll say you were already insured."

I'll admit I didn't know much when I was twenty-one but I wasn't *that* stupid, so we took a train to Rotterdam, bought the insurance and returned. Now we were ready to go.

We tied our duffle bag on to the bike and it acted as a sort of back rest for Donna, put on helmets (which the man who sold us the bike included at no charge when he realized we couldn't afford them), slipped on ponchos to keep dry and we hit the road. Before our wedding we had never spent an entire day and night together; now we could look forward to eighty-eight of them.

We headed east and on our third day out, the Puch suddenly died while I was passing a truck on the German autobahn. I pulled over onto the median where we were trapped by speeding cars and trucks whizzing by. I tried unsuccessfully to restart the bike then reluctantly we began walking toward Hamburg. After only 100 yards, a police car pulled onto the grass next to us and we were scolded in rapid German by two peak capped officers of the law. When they stopped lecturing me, I began explaining my plight to them in English which elicited only blank looks.

"Hmm, this isn't going too well," I said to Donna, "let's try... motorad... kaput!" This was accompanied by a mime impression of a motorcycle driver, followed by my pointing at the disabled vehicle back up the road.

"Ah! Kaput!" one of them repeated as he spotted the bike behind us.

"Kaput," said the other one with a big smile.

They drove us back to the spot and called for help. In a few minutes, a mechanic from the DARC (German Automobile Club) on a yellow motorcycle with a sidecar arrived. He worked on the bike as Donna and I stood with the policemen watching cars go by at a breakneck pace on the speed-limit free superhighway. Donna captured a great picture of the scene with our five dollar camera and soon the mechanic was putting his tools away. He jumped on the kick starter and the engine came back to life.

"What did he do?" Donna asked me.

"I'm not sure but I think he changed the spark plug," I answered.

"Danke Schoen," I said, "How much money?.. er... Wie... viel... Deutche Marks?"

"Nein keiner," the mechanic said with a big smile, "Guten tag."

"How much is that," I asked in Donna's direction.

"I think he said it's free," she replied.

The policeman told me to drive back onto the highway on his signal. He turned on his blue lights and blocked the passing lane until I could get over safely. If it hadn't been for their help, the trip could have taken a very different path.

Motorcycle repair on Autobahn - Hamburg, Germany (1966)

When we arrived in Copenhagen we realized that Europe on ten dollars a day wasn't going to happen. We had no credit cards or access to the little money that we still had in the bank in America, so we did the only sensible thing we could think of... we called home.

Of course we didn't have a phone with us so we went to a Danish government telecommunication center (attached to the post office) and said, "We would like to call America."

The clerk replied, "Okay. You come back on Tuesday and we will have a line open for you."

"Tuesday?" I repeated, "But today is Friday."

"Yes. So you come back on Tuesday. Thirteen hundred hours. Okay?"

"Sure. Okay."

On Tuesday at one, we were told to enter booth number two and sure enough an international operator was waiting. We gave her

Donna's father's phone number. It was eight in the morning in Winthrop. He said he'd send the money.

Before our wedding, Mr. Marukelli had told us he would pay the first year's rent on an apartment.

"Thank you," I said at the time, "I appreciate the offer but I think I'd rather pay my own rent."

(I, of course, actually had no idea how I would do that.)

"Okay," he said, "Then I'll give you five hundred dollars as a wedding present."

"Great," I said.

But our wedding day came and went, and the money never materialized. So now we waited for it to arrive at American Express in Copenhagen. I had recalculated that the trip would likely cost almost fourteen dollars a day so the five hundred additional dollars would be more than enough. It took a few days for the money to appear and when it did... it was $250 short!

"We'll make it work," I said, "I'm not asking him again."

Arriving in Sweden, we discovered that they drove on the left side of the road. At least until January 1, 1967 when Sweden was switching to driving on the right. (Driving was forbidden for eight hours while they made entrances into exits-- and visa versa-- on highways and uncovered already installed road signs.) But for our visit, Donna's job was to keep reminding me to keep to the left, especially after turns and entering roundabouts.

After a few more (expensive and not so warm) days in Scandinavia, we decided to head south instead of continuing to Norway.

To visit Berlin, we had to cross East Germany so we got a visa and after driving a few hours we came to a fork in the road. A large green sign, pointing to the left said (in all caps), "BERLIN", while a smaller blue sign pointing to the right said, "Berlin."

Being unable to confer with Donna sitting on the back of the motorcycle, I decided to go left (the larger sign). After about a mile we came to a heavily armed roadblock. A machine gun wielding soldier looked at our papers and informed us that we were supposed to take the other road.

"This goes to Berlin," he said, "The other road goes to *West* Berlin. You must go back."

So we went back and took the other turn to West Berlin.

The next day we entered East Berlin on the bike through the American checkpoint and drove around. We illegally exchanged some Marks at the street rate (10 to 1 instead of 4 to 1) and had a great (no longer expensive) meal. All around the restaurant were signs telling us we were in a *Worker's paradise* and *No tipping is allowed* and *Capitalism is for the weak*.

After the meal, the tuxedo wearing waiter stood next to me, leaned down and in perfect English whispered with a grin, "Tipping... is okay."

I leaned across to Donna and even though I had never taken a political science course, predicted, "Remember my words, we are going to win the cold war."

Leaving the east sector that evening I was stopped by an East German guard and asked, "Do you have any East German Marks?"

"Yes."

"Would you like to donate them to the East German Red Cross?" she said.

"No."

"Then vee vill take them," she informed me.

So... I donated. The next day I smartened up and after our visit I put some Marks in my sock before we returned through the checkpoint. When asked again if I had any East German Marks, I answered, "No," and was pleasantly surprised that no one noticed how much I was sweating or the obvious limp I had developed. I successfully smuggled the souvenir money out.

The journey across the Alps was awesome but almost too much for the Puch. When my roadside mechanical expertise proved insufficient, we stopped in Innsbruck for repairs. The mechanic put down what he was doing and hoisted our bike onto his bench and replaced the chain which could no longer be adjusted. With the motorbike back on the ground he approached and handed me a slip of paper on which he had written *5 Shillings*.

"Excuse me... five? That can't be right," I said.

We had just arrived in Austria that morning so I wasn't used to Shillings yet but I was pretty sure they were worth four US cents each.

"Twenty cents to repair the motorcycle?"

I tried to get him to keep a twenty Shilling note but he refused, so I handed him a 5 Shilling coin, thanked him and off we drove. We had so many encounters with nice people on the trip, I can only assume it was because I was traveling with a beautiful blue-eyed young woman.

We never got to Venice because a couple we met in Berlin told us it was *over-rated* and it smelled, so we drove down into Italy and along the Riviera into Spain instead. (Since then we have come to love Venice and Donna often says she would like to live there.)

By the time we reached Barcelona, we were on a pretty strict budget. We found an inexpensive hotel in the center of the Ramblas district but we had to figure out how to eat cheaply. Sitting in a cafe in the central plaza we struggled with the menu until a waiter took pity on us and began bringing us little plates of various foods until we were full. It didn't cost much so we did it again the next night also. Like the rooster who thought he caused the sun to rise, we were pretty sure we had just invented tapas. Ah, youth.

We actually found (in France of all places) a hotel owner who wouldn't give us a room because she didn't think we were married! We showed her our wedding rings but that was not nearly good enough to convince her. We showed her the page in Donna's passport where it had been amended (while we were in London) to show her married name but, being written in English, that was still not good enough to convince her. We stood holding our motorcycle helmets, kissed, then looked at the owner and shrugged our shoulders. She reluctantly gave us a room, but remained certain that we were up to no good. The moral police were alive and well in Limoges, France.

The next day we likely introduced sliced cheese to Orleans, France when (in need of picnic food and not possessing a knife) we entered a charcuterie and bought some ham. The owner sliced it on the machine for us as we requested.

"Oh, and deux cent gram of that fromage," Donna said while pointing, "and could you slice it too, please... s'il vous plaît?"

"Qu'est-ce que vous avez dit?" he asked with a puzzled look.

"Slice the cheese... fromage," she repeated as she pointed to the machine.

"Ce?" he asked as put his hand on the machine.
"Oui oui," Donna said emphatically.
"Marie, viens ici," he called out to his wife.
She came out from the back of the store and he spoke to her (in French of course.)
She looked at the machine, then looked at us, shrugged and said, "Americains... ", then whispered something to him before she turned and went into the back room again.
He sliced the small block of cheese muttering something under his breath with each pass of the blade. He wrapped it and put in on the counter.
"Voila," he said when he finished.
We paid, then sat in a park where we drank wine and made sandwiches with wonderful French bread, ham and sliced cheese. I suppose France has never been the same since (I know we haven't been.)
We loved Paris and spent weeks there, sitting in cafes, discovering Humphrey Bogart movies at a student cinema festival and staying in tiny, cheap hotels with worn-out mattresses and a bathroom down the hall; up a half flight of stairs. It was an amazing moment in time.
After three months of one adventure after another we were flying back from London on our aging British Eagle Airlines, MIT charter plane when somewhere over the Atlantic the pilot's voice could be heard on the intercom, "You've probably noticed that one of the propellers has stopped turning," he said.
No one had, but now we certainly did.
"Not to worry," he continued, "This plane was made to fly on two engines, so we really still have more than we need."
Being an MIT crowd, we wanted to believe that physics would triumph over fear and panic, so we pretended that we believed everything would be alright.
Because of a strong head wind and only three engines, what would have normally been an eleven hour flight was closer to sixteen hours. We flew over Boston, then two and a half hours later, landed in New York evoking wild cheers and a familiar voice calling out over the intercom.
"We made it!" the pilot said in apparent disbelief.

We caught a 727 jet in New York and were back in Boston an hour later. The honeymoon was over.

Selective Service

My father pushed a dish of pasta away from his place at the dining room table, almost knocking over a half full glass of red wine.

"Is that what they taught you in that goddamned college?" my father bellowed. Then he gripped the table as if to steady himself and leaned forward, "And what's with that beard--"

"All I said was that the war is a mistake. We have no right to do this to those people--"

"Oh is that so? So now I suppose you're smarter than the President of the United States," he broke in.

"I'm doing what I think is right that's all," I said, instead of answering the question. I let a few seconds pass then continued, "I decided—"

"*You* decided?" my father interrupted in a loud voice, "What about your country?"

"My country's wrong, damn it!" I blurted out louder still.

"Then why don't you go live in Cuba and see how you like it there!" my dad yelled.

I pushed my chair back and stood up.

"What are you talking about? I don't want to live in Cuba."

"Well maybe you should! You certainly don't belong here!" he said.

His body language signaled that the conversation (such as it was) was over. My dad wouldn't talk to me or be seen in public with me after that for a long while.

Just two nights before, I had been sitting, waiting for my appeal hearing at the Winthrop draft board. Mrs. Farrell, the secretary wearing a pink wool sweater pulled over her shoulders, looked older than she probably was and sat behind a large old wooden desk. She looked at me over her glasses, offered me a hard candy from a small fishbowl next to the telephone and then nodded her head toward the oak door with an opaque glass panel.

"They'll see you now," she said.

I sat and looked at the three man draft board sitting across the table, all wearing suits and ties, veterans of one war or another and wondered why a reasonable God would put my fate in their hands.

Mr. Gold had a military style crew cut and owned a dry cleaning business. Mr. Fortezza had no hair, sold insurance and had been a selectman as long as anyone could remember. And Dr. McCormack, the chairman, was eighty-one and more than once mentioned that the members of the board were performing a public duty and not being paid for their services. I found it easy to hate them.

I told them I thought I could do more good as a science teacher than a soldier.

Mr. Gold almost seemed to agree and said, "We *are* trying to beat the Russians to the Moon."

I told them the Vietnamese just wanted to be left alone and weren't a threat to us.

Mr. Fortezza answered, "How would you like it if the communists took over the United States."

"That's my point," I jumped in, "The Vietnamese don't want to be taken over by *us*."

Mr. McCormack asked, "Would you fight someone who was raping your mother?"

I couldn't even speak after that question, I just sighed. It felt totally unreal. We all said what we had to say, but none of us listened; then they asked if I had a final statement.

"I don't know what else to do except to follow my conscience," I said.

"Thank you, that's all. We'll take it under advisement," Mr. McCormack said.

The three men didn't even look up as I left.

The previous week I had been summoned to my pre-induction physical at the South Boston Army Base. Before going I called Flip.

"What do I do now?" I asked.

"Go to the physical but whatever you do, don't sign *anything!*" he said stressing the last word.

"Maybe I won't pass the physical," I said.

"No chance," he said, "They don't have very high standards these days."

"Thanks."

I parked my motorcycle next to a jeep in the army base parking lot and carrying my helmet, went inside a huge gymnasium-like building.

"Strip to your shorts, place your clothes on a bench and carry your valuables in the cloth pouch provided for that purpose," we were told by an army officer who introduced himself as our military escort for the day, "and no one is to speak unless spoken to."

Almost naked, I moved toward the line that was forming.

Our military escort walked up to me and said, "What is *that* doing there on the bench?"

"This? You mean my helmet?" I asked.

"You were told to place your *clothes* on a bench. Is a helmet, *clothes*?"

I wanted to say, "*You're kidding, right?*" but I just shrugged my (bare) shoulders.

"Pick it up and carry it," he ordered.

So I walked, snaking around between rope barriers, for four hours getting inspected, examined and questioned with two or three hundred other potential draftees, while carrying my motorcycle helmet. It was quite a sight and peeing in a cup required my wearing the helmet for a moment or two.

It was "drop your pants," and "stand on one leg" and "read this chart," until at noon our military escort announced, "Chow time gentlemen!" But before we could pick up a metal tray, we had to walk to a table and were told, "Sign the sheet. It releases us from responsibility if you should choke to death."

"We can only hope," I whispered.

When I reached the table I began to read the small print on the sheet (remember I was told not to sign *anything.*)

"What's the hold-up?" our military escort asked as he walked over, "You! With the helmet! Out of the line!" he ordered.

"Me?" I asked.

"Yes you. Out of the line!"

By three o'clock I was starving, but I knew my lawyer would be proud of me.

Finally we came to the last station where they drew blood from your arm. The kid in front of me fainted and they carried him off to the side and laid him on a cot.

"Next," they called, "and do not faint, we only have the one cot."

As ordered, I didn't faint and they took my blood. Then I got dressed and rode home.

To no one's surprise, I both... passed the pre-induction physical, *and*... lost the draft board appeal. Soon a draft card arrived in the mail; I was classified 1-A.

Flip wasn't phased by the news and announced, "Don't worry, we're filing in federal court. They haven't seen anything yet. We'll subpoena the Secretary of Defense if we have to."

I must admit that I didn't share his confidence but at least it would buy some time.

After months of my dad not talking to me (or acknowledging my existence) Donna had had enough. She drove out to Hanscom Airbase, walked into his office while her mother (Mimi) waited in the car. Donna figured that with his co-workers around, he would be more likely to be quiet and listen so she proceeded to read him the riot act.

"Do you know how lucky you are to have a son like him?" Etc... etc.

He tried to argue with her but was completely out of his league. By the time she was finished he apparently saw the error of his ways and within a week we all got together for a meal again. The topic of the Vietnam War or my father's draft deferment during World War II or my beard were never brought up again.

Never.

The Shrink

"Do you mind if I don't sit on the couch?" I asked.
"Sit wherever you like," he said.
It was a bright, sunny afternoon but with the drapes drawn, the room was in twilight, not helped by the dark wood paneling and black leather furniture. I chose the chair opposite his desk.
The doctor was in his forties and had lost a good deal of his hair but was attempting to hide the fact with a comb-over. He straightened his glasses and looked at the small clock sitting in front of him.
"Why did you come here today?" he asked more like a friend than a psychiatrist.
"I don't want to go to Vietnam. I think it's unconscionable what we're doing there. I'm trying to get a deferment but it seems unlikely and if I don't run away to Canada, it could mean jail. People say that's crazy. I'm confused. I have a wife. I think I know what's right but-- I don't know what makes sense anymore. Am I crazy?"
He took the cap off of his pen.
"Let me ask you a few questions," he said calmly then waited for me to relax and settle in the chair.
"Tell me about your mother," he said.
I did.
"How do like being married?" he asked.
I told him.
"What were your friends in grade school like?"
I explained about Victor Dominic.
This went on for thirty minutes. I had taken a few psych courses in college, so most of the questions seemed predictable to me.
Then he asked, "What does your father think about all this?"
"He thinks I'm crazy… and a coward."
"How do you feel about that?"
"I don't know. Maybe I am," I said.
"Which?" he asked.
"Both. Neither. I don't know."

"What do you suppose prison would be like?"

I leaned forward and almost stood up.

"Look, I'm not stupid. But I'm not going to give in… I'm not afraid--"

"Oh?" he interrupted.

I was caught off guard.

"Well... a little. Okay, a lot. But I'm right. And I'm not going to give in."

"If you're so sure you're right, why are you here?" he asked forcefully.

I bit on a fingernail as I answered.

"I guess… truth be told, I have a really hard time believing that I could be right; and everybody else be wrong. Everyone says it's crazy to choose jail. I don't know; what if they're right," I said.

The doctor stood, walked over to the window and pulled the drapes back, letting in the light. Then he moved around to the front of his desk and leaned back against it, facing me. He took off his glasses.

"Look," he said, "We can go on meeting if you like, but let me share something with you. When I was your age, I would have done *anything* to avoid going to Korea. It's the reason I went to graduate school."

He stood up now and walked around as he talked.

"In 1950, they called it a police action… but plenty of young men were dying and we couldn't make heads-or-tails of why. Anyway I-- like you-- wanted no part of it. And I-- like you-- felt that I was right. So I suppose if you're crazy; that makes me crazy. But I can't be crazy… because I'm the psychiatrist."

We both laughed, although the more I thought about it, the less funny it seemed.

I thanked him, left and never went back again.

The Motorcycle File

The phone rang. It was my Mother.

"Ernie," she said with unmistakable concern in her voice, "the FBI wants to talk with you."

"What? What do they want?" I asked.

"He left a number. You should call him," she said, "Promise me you'll call him."

It was April, 1967-- Donna and I were living in a two room apartment on Commonwealth Avenue, the Vietnam War was getting out of control and the draft board had recently notified me that because I had graduated college in January, my draft status was being changed to 1-A (*available for military service*). I applied for a 2-A work deferment as a high school teacher but that was denied. I appealed that decision and lost, so my lawyer and I were about to take the case to Federal Court.

Through a million years of evolution, humans have acquired a willingness in times of need to sacrifice themselves for the "greater good." Where my wife and children are concerned I likely inherited that trait, but in the case of the Vietnam War, Lyndon Johnson's misguided, twisted logic and outright lies left me unconvinced. Some young men enlisted in the military and many acquiesced to being drafted, but a large number stayed in college as long as they could for the deferment, a small number fled to Canada, and some went to prison rather than serve. I felt cornered. The Selective Service System and I seemed to be heading for an unavoidable confrontation with no apparent good outcomes.

And now the FBI wanted to talk to me.

Donna and I had married the previous June, flown to London, hitchhiked for a while and then managed to buy a used Austrian motorcycle in Amsterdam for $190 (We couldn't afford helmets so the dealer took pity on us and included them for free.) I had never been on a motorcycle before, learned to ride it in the parking lot the day we bought it, and for the next three months we drove all over Europe. The plan was to sell the bike in Paris before catching a train to London for the return flight home, but we were unable to sell it in France without an exporter's license. So we took a chance and rode it to Belgium to try again. No luck there either. So as time ran out and we boarded the train, I signed the registration papers and gave the bike to a young American student. He thanked me and the last I saw of the bike, he was standing next to it in the Brussels's train station parking lot.

Sitting on the night boat-train to London I turned to Donna and said,"I was really counting on selling the bike. We'll be lucky if we have money for a cab when we get home."

"So... we'll walk," she said.

When we arrived back in Boston I had twenty dollars in my wallet. We were met at the airport by my parents, so we didn't need a cab. I have no memory of where we spent the night, but the next day we were on the MIT campus where Donna got a job in Amar Bose's office (Bose Speakers), I got back in school for my final semester and then three days later we moved into our new apartment in the Back Bay! That was six months ago.

Now I had the FBI to deal with. I dialed the number Mom had given me and asked for Agent Mills. I told him who I was.

"Mr. Cataldo, we would like to talk with you," he said, "Can you come in to our Government Center Office?

"What's it about?"

"We just need to talk with you," he replied politely.

"About what? Do I need a lawyer or anything?"

"We just need to talk with you, that's all." He was getting a little exasperated. "Ninth floor. Just ask for Agent Mills."

"What's it--"

He hung up.

I immediately called Flip to see if he had any idea what this could be about.

He was a year older than me, had just gotten his first real job at a big downtown law firm and was even more idealistic than I was (which was not easy.)

"What's up?" he asked when his secretary told him it was me.

I recounted what agent Mills had said, then I added, "You know how you told me that the FBI might have our phone calls bugged? And you know how once in a while on the phone you say '*Fuck J. Edgar Hoover'* just to piss them off? Well... maybe they really were listening."

"Let them listen! You gotta love the First Amendment," he said, then getting to the business at hand, "It is a little puzzling but... go meet with them and let me know what they say... and keep your answers short and truthful... and whatever you do, *don't sign anything*!"

"Okay, thanks," I said and hung up before he could test our First Amendment rights again.

Armed with Flip's advice, I exited the elevator onto the ninth floor of the JFK Federal building and passed the posters of the *ten most wanted* criminals in the United States. I didn't recognize anyone so I continued to the FBI front desk.

"I'm here to see Agent Mills," I announced.

Behind the receptionist were endless cubicles with walls that didn't quite reach the ceiling. She directed me to one. It had no door, but next to the opening was a small plaque that read, *L.S. Mills, Special Agent.* I cleared my throat.

"Yes? Can I help you?" he looked up and asked.

He was about thirty-five years old with crew cut brown hair and wore a short sleeve white shirt and tie. His jacket with an American flag pin on the lapel was hanging on a hook next to a picture of Lyndon Johnson. I had the beginnings of a beard and was wearing a sweatshirt with a peace symbol printed on the back.

"I'm Ernest Cataldo," I admitted, "We spoke on the phone."

I sat down as he found a folder and opened it on his desk. He turned over a few pages then stopped and looked at me.

"Do you own a motorcycle?" he asked.

"No."

He thought a moment then said, "Did you *ever* own a motorcycle?"

"Yes," I said. *Uh-oh*, I thought.

He smiled and quickly asked, "Where is it now?"

I got the feeling that he already knew the answer. I tried to keep my reply short.

"Well, the last time I saw it, over six months ago, it was in a parking lot at the train station in Brussels, Belgium."

He looked at the folder then said, "It's still there... and the Brussels police would like to know what you'd like to do with it."

I was completely unprepared, but surprised myself and quickly came up with an idea.

"Do you think they have a widows and orphans fund?" I asked.

"I'll bet they do," he replied with a grin on his face.

"Then maybe they could sell the bike and use the proceeds for that. What do you think?" I said.

"I think that's a great idea," he said as he wrote a few lines on a sheet of paper then slid it toward me, "just sign below."

"How in the world did the FBI get involved in this?" I inquired as I signed.

"Interpol," he said.

"Interpol, wow," I said. But what I really wanted to say was, *What else is in that folder?"*

We shook hands and I left, again passing the *ten most wanted* posters. Walking home through the Boston Common, I realized just how much I missed having a motorcycle.

I arrived back at our two room apartment; two rooms being a generous description to be sure. One and a half would have been more accurate. It was pretty cramped with just Donna and me but not long after I began teaching, our family grew. We found ourselves with a foster child (well... foster teenager) named Zoe. She was a student in my algebra I class and was so frightfully withdrawn that I inquired about her situation and found out that she had been forceably removed from her home by a police SWAT team when she was six and her mother committed to an institution. Zoe was a ward of the State and had been placed in a series of foster homes, been abused, had an abortion *and* given birth to a baby that was then put up for adoption. She was now all of *sixteen year old* and the only place the State could find for her to stay was the mental health facility at Mass General Hospital.

At the end of class that day I asked her to stay behind.

"What's it like living at MGH?"

"It's hard to do homework there. People are always screaming," she said without emotion, "And they lock the door at night and don't unlock it until morning."

"How would you like to live with me and my wife?"

"Okay," she replied as if it were a question she was often asked.

Donna was unsure at first. She was only three years older than

Zoe but agreed it was the right thing to do... at least for a while.

We rented a bed and let her have our "second room" which was not much more than a large closet with a window. I contacted her social worker, a woman barely out of college (not unlike myself), who agreed to meet Donna and me at our apartment.

Miss Social Worker resisted the idea of Zoe staying with us.

"Oh no. We never allow a placement with a child's teacher," she told us, "Never."

"She can't stay where she is," I pushed, "Do you have some other reasonable place for her to live?"

"We've been trying for months to place her. We're even looking into some southern states. Alabama might take her but even there, with her past--"

"Then let her stay with my wife and me," I interrupted.

"I'm afraid we can't allow that," Miss Social Worker replied.

"Well, until you get a court order," I said, "she's staying right here."

Zoe (1968)

She picked up her briefcase, went to the door and turned, "I'll see what I can do," she said and left.

The next day the phone rang. It was Miss Social Worker.

"My supervisor said we'll give it a trial period," she informed me.

They checked on us a few times but soon the Child Welfare Department gave in, made it official and began sending a monthly allowance for Zoe. We went right out and bought her a bed. She was basically a good kid and tried, but it was a real struggle for a young couple to have another person in the house, let alone a teenage person (and a teenager with a difficult past at that.) We had to convince her to wear underwear, to not put her feet on the dining room table and to smoke less-- just to name a few things. But we soon got used to having her around; and life went on.

A few months passed; then Flip called me and said, "I want you to go to the draft board and pick up a copy of everything in your file."

"Everything? Can I do that?" I inquired.

"Yes, of course you can. The law says they have to keep everything pertaining to the case. I've sent them dozens of letters, magazine clippings, newspaper articles-- I even sent them a manila envelope with peanut butter in it. We have a court order. If they haven't kept everything, it will help our case in the coming months."

"Peanut butter?" I said, "Really?"

"Just get the files, okay?" he said.

"Okay."

I called Mrs. Farrell at the draft board in Winthrop and told her what I needed. We had come to know each other pretty well in the past year as my case worked its way along and she said she had received the order. She didn't seem fazed by the request.

"Come by on Wednesday afternoon," she told me.

On Wednesday I went up the stairs to the second floor office and greeted Mrs. Farrell. She looked dismayed.

"I'm so sorry," she said sincerely, "I don't have it all together yet. There was a lot more material than I expected."

"Oh," I muttered and avoided her eyes. I imagined peanut butter everywhere.

"Can you come back in a few hours?" she asked.

"Well, I have to pick up my daughter at four, so--"

"Daughter? You have a daughter?" she interrupted.

"Well, not a real daughter. You know, a foster daughter," I explained.

Mrs. Farrell looked puzzled then put her hand up to her face and adjusted her glasses.

"A foster daughter? Placed by Child Welfare? By the State of Massachusetts?" she asked.

"Yes."

She pushed her chair back and stood up.

"Then... you are entitled to a fatherhood deferment," she

proclaimed, "3-A classification."

"Are you sure?" I asked.

She looked at me over her glasses with an expression that said, "*I know more about the Selective Service System than anyone in this town and if I say you're 3-A... you're 3-A*"

She certainly knows more about the Selective Service System than my lawyer, I thought.

Soon I had a draft card that said I was 3-A (*registrant with child*). And just like that, a weight was lifted off of me. Canada, army, conscientious objector, Vietnam, prison... were just words again.

Winter came to an end and I decided I had gone long enough without a motorcycle. I bought a red 250 cc Yamaha (and we still had the helmets we were given in Holland). Living in the city center and walking to work, it had been a necessary but difficult choice to sell our beloved TR4, so the motorcycle was our only set of wheels but still it was great fun.

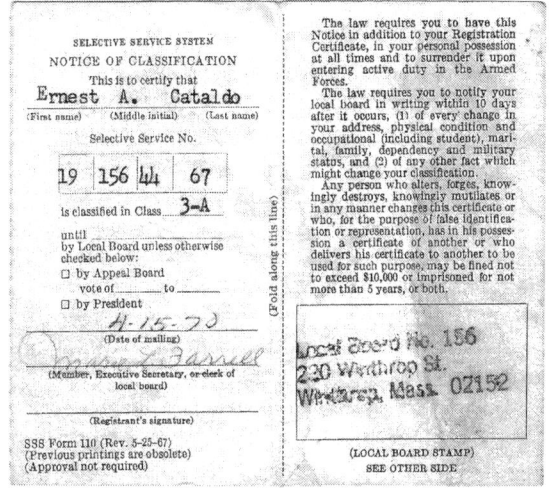

My 3-A "fatherhood" deferment (1970)

Then things changed a little. The three of us moved to Beacon Hill and Donna announced there would soon be a fourth.

All spring and summer of 1970 Donna and I created somewhat of a stir by riding everywhere (including family dinners and birth classes) on the motorcycle *and* we were planning to bike to the hospital as well. It all seemed perfectly logical to us at the time. After all, it was our only motor vehicle and the doctor, when asked, said it was all right with him, putting Donna's fears to rest by citing that old adage, "You can shake an apple tree but the apples won't fall until they're ready."

That came to be known as the "*ripe apple theory*" when our

parents and assorted acquaintances discussed the possibility of a pothole in the road causing the delivery to commence without warning.

Fortunately, it all became academic when the motorcycle was stolen from in front of our house by persons unknown, just weeks before the birth. I jokingly said that I suspected it was the work of my mother-in-law, Mimi, but more likely it was just nature's way of making sure I grew up in time to be a father.

As it turned out, we took a cab to the hospital the day Zac was born, and I haven't been on a motorcycle since. I admit that I missed it at first but I have no regrets. Well... maybe one.

I still wouldn't mind knowing what else is in my FBI file.

Mrs. Miller

Mrs. Miller wasn't important. She was just the cook at my fraternity house. In fact, until I was the treasurer and had to write out her check each week, I didn't even know her first name was Rosa.

To and from classes, I used the back entrance, so every day while passing the kitchen I would be greeted by a smiling Mrs. Miller as she prepared her famous Shepard's pie or stirred a large pot of soup.

She was tall, thin and wore her hair back in a bun. She was always quick with a compliment or advice.

"My... don't you look like somethin' today," she'd say, or "Lord, it's cold out. Best button up."

If I had to miss supper, she would put aside a slice of her wonderful lemon meringue pie for me.

The next morning on my way out she would reach in the refrigerator, hold it up and say, "I know you likes the pie," and laugh.

She was right about that.

If the Red Sox were playing, she was listening on the radio.

"I sure love the baseball," she told me once, "since I was a child."

She cooked two meals a day, six days a week for us and had been doing so since 1938.

She cooked, and Joseph served.

As she told it, Joseph was hired as the butler two months after she arrived, "And he's been no good ever since," she would say. Then she laughed so hard you couldn't help but laugh with her.

First term, senior year I was elected treasurer. Until then I hadn't given a thought to how bills were paid or where the money came from... or went. So I was sitting in the treasurer's closet learning my new duties and looking over the books when I came to the *accounts payable*.

"*This* is what she makes for a week?" I said aloud, "This must be a mistake."

It was no mistake. She and Joseph made the minimum wage... $1.25 an hour!

"They take home forty-eight dollars a week, with the overtime," I said at the next chapter meeting, "That's absurd. You and I are here for four short years... they're always here. They are the fraternity."

When confronted with the facts, the members were shamed into raising the salaries despite some opposition.

"Our house bills will go up," some nincompoop said.

"So?" I eloquently countered.

We raised the salaries and someone figured out that they were both also eligible for Social Security payments. Mrs. Miller required a little paperwork but Joseph was another matter.

"Joseph, they need proof of your age. Do you have a birth certificate, driver's license, anything?"

"No sir, "he said, "but I got this picture of me an' my regiment in the big war."

You could see young Joseph clear as day in the front row. He had hardly changed.

We took that official army picture of him and his all black combat unit, taken in 1918, to the Social Security office (the business and political science majors in the house were especially helpful) and they sent us to the Department of the Army but eventually Joseph got his Social Security payments and a military stipend. Joseph was clearly proud of being recognized for his service.

One day in the kitchen he told me, "I wish I could be buried in that old uniform but I done give it to Mrs. Miller to make them bags."

"Bags?" I said.

Mrs. Miller explained.

"I been living with my sister since we was girls," she said, "and we sew up bags for the Red Cross for the soldiers in the wars. We made up some nice one's from that old uniform of his; b'sides, look at him, it wouldn't fit him no more."

Then she laughed so hard you couldn't help but laugh with her.

I spent a few minutes with Mrs. Miller whenever I could and got to know her a little better. I found out that she was born in

Alabama, had no formal education but she knew the ways of the world.

"Promise me you won't eat them hot dogs," she said.

"Okay, but why?" I asked.

"Because I worked in a meat packin' plant and I know what's in 'em!"

Then came that laugh.

One afternoon while sitting in the kitchen, I said, "You must have seen a lot over the years."

"I watched that Mystic Bridge be built but I ain't never been on it," she said as if it had been on her mind.

"Never? How do you get out of town?" I asked naively.

"I only been outside of Boston once since I was a girl," she said, "Took a bus to my daddy's funeral in Montgomery in 1951."

She got quiet for a moment, then said, "But I'd love to see Montreal. I hear it's really somethin'."

The next day, as I walked by, I heard Mrs. Miller's radio blaring, "...*opposite field home run for Carl Yastrzemski. Clear over the left field wall!*"

I ducked into the kitchen to listen.

"Oh, I'd love to see that," she said.

"See what?" I asked, without thinking.

"That wall. It must be somethin'," she said.

"Don't tell me you've never been to Fenway Park," I said.

"Never," she replied, "And I don't have no TV neither."

At the next chapter meeting...

"Gentlemen, we *are* paying them a living wage now but I think there is more we can do...," I began.

I picked Mrs. Miller up in my TR4 roadster and drove her over the Mystic River Bridge.

"Oh Lord...," she said as we neared the middle of the span, "...you can take me now, if you wants to."

We bought her tickets to a Red Sox game and a few of us accompanied her. It was easy to get great seats in those days and she really enjoyed it, except when I ate the hot dog.

We bought her and Joseph each a small television. He kept his in his little room off of the kitchen.

In the spring we sent Mrs. Miller and her sister on an overnight bus trip to Montreal. Time was flying by and I was being tugged away from my life on Beacon Street. I was running out of the house to turn in my undergrad thesis when I noticed something in my mail slot. It was a postcard and it had a picture of a flower sticking up out of the snow and the word "Canada" printed on the front. On the back was written, "*With Love, from Rosa.*"

I got a great engineering education at MIT but I learned a whole lot more about life from Mrs. Rosa Miller.

Odd Jobs

My sophomore year at MIT was coming to an end and there was no way I wanted to live at home for the next two months, so I planned to room at the fraternity and I was about to interview for a summer job near the campus. I stood in the lobby of the Pledge of Allegiance Building on Columbus Avenue looking up at the directory: *Pastoriza Electronics - Basement level* it read.

I entered Jim Pastoriza's office and it was clear that he was a hands-on manager; his office was a mess. Electronic equipment, cardboard boxes and papers covered every horizontal surface, including the seat he told me to sit in.

"Just put those on the floor," he said when he saw me hesitate at the chair. "Joe Mammola speaks highly of you."

I sat fidgeting in the chair and he noticed me looking at the diplomas behind him; one from MIT and one from Harvard.

Glancing over his shoulder he said, "I met Joe at MIT; great place."

"What did you study at Harvard?" I asked.

"Let me ask *you* a question," he said, apparently ignoring mine. "My roommate at Harvard came in one day and began packing his bags. I asked him what he was doing and he said he was leaving because he had ideas he wanted to get on with. He said he was wasting his time. I told him that if he left Harvard, he would never amount to anything."

Jim Pastoriza stood up and came around the desk.

"His name was Edwin Land," he said, "...Polaroid?"

He stuck out his hand and said, "I'm a terrible judge of people so I'm going to take Joe's word for it. Welcome aboard."

I stood and shook his hand.

"Thank you," I said, "but... what was your question?"

"Can you start today?"

"Sure," I answered.

"Good. Go down the hall and ask for Richie," he said, pointing the way.

Richie apparently had no idea I was coming or who I was (or

what I was there for) so he showed me the conference room, pointed at a 10 foot wide bookcase and told me to "put these catalogs in order."

"In order?" I said.

"You know; A before B; that sort of thing."

Then he left.

I spent ten minutes rethinking my career choice and moving a few things around. I found a road atlas, an issue of Popular Mechanics and even a menu from a Chinese restaurant amid hundreds of new and old parts catalogs. Then just when I was going to give up, an odd looking young man came in. He was thirty-ish with long stringy blond hair but bald on top. I thought he looked like a character in a Dicken's novel.

"You must be Ernie," he said, "I'm Dave. What have they got you doing?"

I told him and added, "I don't know which end is up."

"That's what she said," he replied. Then he opened the door to the hall, "Forget this. No one ever looks at them. Follow me."

He led me further down the hall to a small room with a drafting table.

"Layout the front panel, the switches and such, for our new analog to digital converter," he said, "so manufacturing can make a prototype."

He walked away saying, "It's easy. There's the template and just use the schematic."

I studied the schematic and figured out what controls would be needed on the front.

An hour later Dave returned, looked at my panel layout, and asked, "Where are the lights?"

"The pilot light is right there," I answered, pointing.

"No, no, the *blinking* lights! How will they know if it's working if there are no blinking lights?

I shrugged.

"Haven't you ever seen Star Trek?" he asked.

"Yes, but that isn't real, is it?"

"That's what she said," he interjected, "Listen, the Air Force is spending a fortune on these. They like blinking lights. So we give 'em blinking lights. Simple."

A few weeks later the prototype was on my bench (with blinking lights added) ready for testing. I was told to see if it met the Air Force specs. I heated it in an oven, cooled it in a CO_2 freezer and spun it on a turntable. Now the spec said it had to survive a plane crash event of eight G's.

I asked Dave, "How will I do that?"

"Up to the roof!" he exclaimed as he jumped up and led the way.

We dropped it three stories to the pavement below (twice to be sure.) It wasn't pretty, but back on the bench... it still worked!

The following summer I returned to Pastoriza but they had moved to Newton Lower Falls. I had my own parking space, more responsibilities and Dave now had a pony tail. We also had a new head engineer named Russell, a quintessential absent minded, nerdy engineer. He walked around sporting a pocket protector, wearing a clip-on bow tie and uttering. "Hell's bells," constantly. Every morning Russell would pull into his parking space and collide with the building; sometimes just a touch but often a good whack. One morning Dave put a metal trash can in Russell's space but he simply crushed it before hitting the building. We all heard and felt the impact inside.

"Nothing seems to stop him," I said with a snicker.

"That's what she said," said Dave.

Occasionally Jim, Russell, Dave and I would go out to lunch nearby. It was usually painfully awkward with everyone quietly solving some problem in their head or talking about some deadline they weren't going to meet at work. One day, to break the routine, I told a long, funny (at least I thought it was funny) story. After I delivered the punchline (which was something like, "...if I knew it was so long, I would have stayed home,"), Dave said, "That's what she said,"; Russell said, "Hell's bells" and Jim reached in his pocket, pulled out a notepad and said, "That was a good one. Is it okay if I write it down?"

Those lunches were definitely one of the reasons why I didn't pursue an engineering career.

. . .

On my return from our honeymoon, I still needed a couple of courses to graduate from MIT. Donna had taken a job as a secretary in Amar Bose's section in the electrical engineering department and I figured that with such a light load I could get a part time job and help out. The undergrad employment office sent me to the Sensory Aid Center on Main Street, a lab that designed aids for the blind. I worked with Murray Bernstein, a mechanical engineer who seemed to have two ideas to solve any problem. When a small factory in Brooklyn, where blind and deaf people were employed making brooms, was threatened with closure by the fire department, Murray came up with a fire alarm system that allowed them to stay open. He took an electric toothbrush motor and put it and a small radio receiver, in a case the size of a pack of cigarettes. One was put in each employee's pocket and vibrated if there was a fire alarm. Ropes led from each work station to the exits. Great engineering; simple and ingenious, I thought.

When I heard the problem, *my* first thought was, *How in the world do you teach someone who's deaf and blind to make a broom?*

The lab was headed by a Dr. Dulong, who during World War Two in France was made blind by the Nazis performing medical experiments. He mostly kept to himself except when anyone walked by his office, he prided himself on his ability to call out their name. Murray often tried to imitate the gait of others to fool him, but rarely did.

"Mur-ray" the boss would call out in his thick French accent as Murray passed by trying to mimic my walk.

"In-cre-dibleh, how deed you know it waz mee?" Murray would tease in his fake French accent.

"I'm blind, not an imbecile," he would say, "Now get back to work."

We had blind volunteers test out various inventions but most were not well received. At the time, cameras and other electronics were bulky and the volunteers felt that wearing them, made it obvious that they were blind. They preferred a seeing-eye dog to our devices (like that didn't make it obvious they were blind), but I have to admit the dogs were amazing and nicer to have around than a laser positioning device the size of a coffee can worn on your head.

At lunch we would eat at the F&T, an old fashioned diner in

Kendall Square. Mr. Fox and Mr. Tishman were the owners, cooks and showmen behind the counter. I would place an order just for the fun of hearing them.

"Mr. Tishman, this gentleman says he wants to know if we any have custard pie today," Fox would call out.

"Ask him why he wants to know, Mr. Fox."

"I think he wants to *buy* a piece Mr. Tishman. He looks hungry to me."

"Then what are you waiting for Mr. Fox? Tell him yes for heaven sake."

Of course, that was then... now it's a Starbucks or a Bank of America.

I stayed at the Sensory Aid Center until September 1967, when after taking a few State required courses at BU, I began teaching math and science at Shaw Prep, a few blocks from our apartment. On my first day there, I met with Mr. Roach, the headmaster. I disliked him from the first moment but I have to admit, he gave me some of the best advise I ever got.

"Don't ever make a threat you aren't prepared to back up. Or these kids will eat you alive."

Words to live by.

A week in, I gave my first geometry quiz and everyone in the class aced it. The next morning I saw Kathy Hogan leaning against the wall in the hall.

"Morning Kathy. I corrected the tests last night and you guys all did well. It's getting across," I said cheerfully.

"Boy! You gotta be kidding," she said as she rolled her eyes back in her head, "How dumb can you be?"

"What are you talking about?" I asked.

"You had the test in your desk drawer yesterday morning before you gave it... right? With the answer sheet... right?"

"Yes, how did--"

"Duh... We all had a copy of the thing by nine o'clock. If you're going to be a teacher, you can't be so dumb."

More words to live by, and gradually, I slowly did get less dumb.

It was an interesting place.

It's where I met our foster daughter who lived with us for four years.

It's where I met Dr. Cassiano, the language teacher from Romania. He spoke a dozen languages fluently including German and Russian, because his homeland was taken over by both those countries in his lifetime.

It's where I met George McDonough, the English teacher. He was a pilot in the Marine reserves and although not technically true, I credit him with saving my life. Billy Grossman walked into my classroom at the end of the day and stood, arms by his sides, next to my desk where I was sitting correcting papers.

"My father says I can't fail algebra. If I do he'll kill me," Billy said quietly.

"I'm afraid you flunked the final, Billy," I said before looking up.

That's when I noticed that Billy was holding a gun down by his side.

"Billy, let's... stay calm. Maybe we can think of ways to get your grade..."

I rambled on while watching the gun closely. A student walking by my door, saw the scene and ducked into the next room where Mr. McDonough taught. Mr. D. burst in through the connecting door between our rooms and strode quickly toward my desk speaking forcefully, "Billie, give me that gun!"

As Billie turned to face him, Mr. D. grabbed the gun from his hand.

I tested my legs to see if I could stand, then did.

"Not loaded," Mr. D. said contemptuously, "Let's all take a walk and see Mr. Roach, shall we."

Billie explained to the police that it was his father's gun and unfortunately Billie did flunk algebra (and didn't return to the school.) His dad owned a sporting goods store and Billie ended up working there.

I thanked Mr. McDonough and he told me, "If that happens again, look him in the eyes; don't look at the gun."

Still more words to live by. Teaching wasn't as easy as I thought it would be.

It's where I met Errol Thomas, who was hired as a second math teacher when the school expanded but was about to be laid off in September of 1971. That's when I decided I needed a change. I liked teaching and loved the kids but it was hard to keep it fresh and not just rely on what I had done before. So I left Shaw Prep, Errol stayed on and we are still great friends.

I had a one year old son and no job, so, of course, I decided to go to Europe. We drove around in a little white Renault 4 for three months while I considered what to do next with my life.

Wild Bill

By 1968, I had been living in Boston for six years and thought I knew my way around, but I had no idea where the city morgue was.

"I'll grab a cab," I said, "He'll know where it is. What should I wear?"

"You're kidding, right?" Donna answered.

"Yeah. I guess," I replied as I pulled on my sweater.

I descended the stairs from our second floor Commonwealth Avenue apartment past streams of the *"Police Line - Do Not Cross"* tape that blocked the elevator. The horrific odor of the past few days had been replaced by the almost equally unpleasant smell of disinfectant.

I hailed a cab and arrived at an alley entrance of Boston City Hospital. Above the double doors at the end was a sign reading, "Suffolk County Morgue - Ring Bell For Entry."

"There's a joke there somewhere," I said as I paid, then exited the cab.

The taxi driver didn't respond and drove off. I took a deep breath and rang the bell.

...

The odor was first noticed three or four weeks ago but because our apartment was on the second floor we seldom took the elevator so it was only when visiting our friend, Toddy, upstairs that we even were aware of it at the beginning. In a week or so the smell was bad enough that we called the management company, who hung those little tree shaped car deodorizers in the lift compartment. That only worked briefly. Soon the odor was evident everywhere in the hall and eventually over the past few days became overwhelming. That's where things stood when I set off to work that morning.

When I arrived back home at 3:30 that afternoon, I saw two police cars and and a black van out front. On the side of the van it read *Suffolk County Coroner*.

"What's happening?" I asked a policeman.

"Do you live here?"
"Yes. Second floor. What happened?" I asked again.
"There was a body in the elevator shaft," he said.
Oh my God... Wild Bill! I thought.

. . .

Mrs. Grant Borden and her two sons, William and David lived on the third floor across the hall from Toddy. Mrs. Borden was the gray haired, matronly author of a local travel book. She was quiet and kept mostly to herself. In fact the longest conversation we ever had was when she told me how fortunate I was to have moved into the building when I did.

"The three previous winters it has been so cold in this building," she revealed, "and all our complaints were ignored. But this year has been very comfortable. You are so lucky.".

I didn't tell her that after we moved in last September I had picked the lock on the central hall thermostat and moved the temperature up, while bending the indicator back so all looked the same. So much for luck.

Her younger son David was twelve and just a plain sixth grade boy; while William was nineteen and just plain weird. They lived across the hall from Toddy, who's boyfriend, Flip had given William the nickname 'Wild Bill'. It stuck and everyone in the building referred to him that way (except his mother.)

David was at school all day while Bill crouched on a landing in the stairway and recited Bible passages as people passed. David was a medium height and build with brown hair; Bill was tall (when he wasn't crouching), gaunt and had an unkempt head-full of white speckled-brown hair.

"Do you believe in Jesus? He tells me all things," he might say as he stood with hands on his knees swaying from side to side. It could be pretty spooky.

Late one night we heard a scream from upstairs. Half the building arrived as Toddy stood at her doorway in her bathrobe, obviously upset.

"He was in there," she sobbed, "Standing over me. Wild Bill what's-his-name."

We went in her apartment. There was no one there, but the

window onto the fire escape was open and the screen missing. We knocked on Mrs. Borden's door and Bill answered.

"I was only doing what the voices told me," he said, as he rocked back and forth.

"What voices, Bill. Who told you?" someone asked.

"The voices in the refrigerator," he replied.

Someone said, "Okay; that's it. Let's call the police!"

"No," Toddy said, "No don't. He's harmless... just creepy that's all."

Then, a few days later, Bill disappeared. I was pretty used to him by then but I have to admit it was kind of pleasant in the building without him around.

I saw Mrs. Borden in the entrance soon after, and asked, "Where's Bill, I haven't seen him for a few days."

"Oh... he's visiting friends out of town," she said.

Thank you Jesus, I thought.

...

I pushed the button and heard the bell ring inside the morgue.

A middle aged man in a once white uniform, opened the door six inches, stared at me for a second then said, "I.D.?"

I reached for my wallet.

"No," he said, "Are you here to I.D. a body?"

"Yes."

"Step inside. What's the case number?" the attendant asked.

"I don't know," I answered, "The-- his-- mother asked me to..."

"Are you related?"

"A family friend," I lied.

"The deceased's name?"

"Borden. William Borden."

"Okay, follow me," he said. He referred to a list on his desk then muttered, "Case 561."

He took me to a vastly over-sized file cabinet, slid out a drawer and I could feel the temperature in the room drop.

I had seen this on TV before but under *this* sheet was a *real* corpse.

"Ever do this before?" he asked in a friendly way.

"No. Mrs. Borden asked me if I'd come and identify her son,

that's all. She said she couldn't face it."

"Well, brace yourself; it's not a pretty sight. He's been dead at least four weeks. Take a hold of this bag."

I took the paper bag from him. I already didn't feel well.

"I'll roll the sheet down slowly and when you're sure it's him, say so. And don't worry about throwing up; you won't be the first. All I ask is that you use the bag; we want to keep this fella clean."

Morgue humor, I thought, *just what I need.*

Gradually as the sheet moved down, familiar white speckled hair came into view.

The attendant halted and advised me, "The skin has discolored. Ignore the color."

He continued to expose the face.

"It's him It's him," I said and looked away.

He pulled the sheet up, slid the drawer in and went to his desk.

"Write you name and address and sign here," he said.

I walked home, taking lots of deep breaths and tried to lose the image.

. . .

David and I got a little closer after Bill's death. David helped me work on my motorcycle and I took him for rides where we would sometimes sneak a doughnut. Once in a while he came downstairs for help with his math homework. He seemed okay.

Then I came home one afternoon to find a broken pane of glass at the building's front entry door and a trail of blood leading up the stairs. I followed the blood drops to the Borden's door, which was ajar and I heard a voice in the bedroom. I couldn't make out what was being said.

Mrs. Borden, are you okay?" I called out.

No answer, just the voice. So I looked into the bedroom and beyond into the bathroom. There was David in the tub seemingly unconscious with Mrs. Borden hunched over him, praying. There was blood everywhere. She didn't seem to notice me.

"Have you called an ambulance," I asked trying to remain calm.

"No need," she said without looking up, "Jesus will find a way."

"Well, let's give him a little help!" I shouted as I looked around frantically for her phone. I met the ambulance downstairs and led them up. Mrs. Borden only resisted for a moment, then stepped aside and they rushed David to Boston City Hospital. Two days later I saw him outside on the stoop with his arm in a sling but apparently otherwise okay.

"Thank you," he said to me, "You know, sometimes my mom gets a little... you know-- funny."

"Don't worry about it," I said, "just get better."

He gave me a long, one armed hug.

"You're going to be fine," I assured him.

I certainly hope I was right.

We moved to Beacon Hill soon after that and I never saw David again.

Grandparents

All four of my grandparents were dead by the time I was twelve. My paternal grandmother died during the Spanish Flu epidemic of 1918, ten years after she and my grandfather, Ernesto, had immigrated to America. Her five year old son, Alfred (my father), watched her as she was being carried from their home on a stretcher to a waiting ambulance. She called Alfred over and put her lips next to his ear.

"You take care of your father. And promise me you won't let another woman in his bed while I'm away," she whispered.

"I promise Mama," he said.

Alfred never saw his mother again.

Six months later, Ernesto arrived home one evening with a woman and announced to his children, "This is your new mother."

Then they walked upstairs and into the bedroom.

Alfred went into the kitchen, picked up a knife and climbed the stairs. He entered the bedroom and attempted to keep his promise to his mother. He tried to stab the woman! My grandfather's reaction was swift and brutal. No police were called and no psychologist consulted. As you might expect, Alfred and his stepmother never got along and he couldn't wait to get out of that house. At age sixteen, after one too many beatings, he moved in with an aunt. My dad reconciled with his father later in life, after I was born, but I was told that I was named after my father's older brother, Ernesto, not after my grandfather. I can believe it.

My dad didn't talk much about his father, but he did tell of the night Joe Kennedy (JFK's father) came to the house. It was about 1928, Joe was an officer at the South Boston Savings Bank and the City of Boston was about to build the Sumner Tunnel. Apparently Joe got wind of the plan and financed my grandfather, who quietly bought up the land (old tenements mostly, on the East Boston side), before the plan was made public. In time, the city bought the land, but my grandfather would only accept cash, so Joe Kennedy came to the house with a straw suitcase to divide up the money. Two for Joe and one for Grandpa until the $300,000 was gone. (That's about four million in today's dollars.)

    I remember my grandfather, Ernesto, as a giant of a man. He was 6 foot 5 inches tall and weighed 250 pounds. I was always straining my neck to look at him and I never recall him coming down to my level. I didn't like him much and certainly didn't look forward to seeing him (or his wife for that matter.) He died when I was about ten years old. In his will, he left me (and each of the grandchildren) a thousand dollars, but my dad's step-mother and step-brothers sued and got the will vacated.

    My maternal grandfather, Pasquale Pepicelli, was a stone mason. He had a slight build, white hair and mustache and often wore a skimmer straw hat. I was five when I last saw him. He left my grandmother after she became blind from diabetes, and he returned to Italy. Years later on his death bed, his last request was to be buried next to his wife back in America. I remember all my aunts and uncles getting the money together so his body could be flown home to be interred here. Even at eleven years of age, I thought they were all nuts!

    What's the matter, they couldn't dig a hole in the ground in Italy? I wondered.

. . .

    My mother's mother was a typical Italian Nonna. She cooked, cleaned the house, wore dowdy house-dresses, grew spearmint out in the garden and most amazing of all-- to me as a five year old-- she could set the table. No matter where I sat for lunch, she would place the plate of food right in front of me even though she was totally blind! I still don't know how she did it.

    I liked Nonna but she had those opaque, gray eyes, and I didn't really understand what 'being blind' was like, so I was a little frightened of her too.

    My mom and her sisters and brothers took turns to be sure someone was almost always at Grandma's apartment, so I spent an afternoon a week there playing on the back porch while Mom was getting groceries or the like. I had to content myself with a few toy trucks and the noisy mantle clock that chimed every fifteen minutes: once at quarter past the hour, twice at the half hour, and three times at quarter to the hour; and of course it chimed the hour.

Sometimes I would sit and wait for it to click and start whirring so I could count the bells. I wasn't very proficient at telling time yet but it was something to do.

One rainy day when I was particularly bored I went and sat next to grandma at the kitchen table.

"Grandma, why don't you have a television?" I asked.

"You a nice-a boy," she answered.

What kind of answer is that? I wondered. It didn't occur to me that she had no idea what a television was (and couldn't see it if she did.)

RCA mirror lid TV (1948)

I, on the other hand, couldn't imagine not having a TV. The previous year (1948) we got the first television on our block and my friends, cousins, and I would gather round it when transmission began late in the afternoon. That first TV was mounted in its cabinet with the picture tube facing up and viewed via an angled mirror, due to the belief that the 'cathode rays' emanating from the screen would be harmful. I guess RCA didn't care that much about my cousin Dotty and her family, who lived upstairs. At three o'clock, the hissing static gave way to a test pattern that stayed on for the first half-hour so you could adjust your set, (I suppose watching the test pattern on the TV was good practice for watching the mantle clock at grandma's) then the national anthem played, followed by the Kate Smith variety show and *finally... finally...* Howdy Doody. So obviously, you can see why, on the days that I was stuck at grandma's house, it was important to be back home by three.

I was pushing a Tonka dump truck on the back porch and heard the clock chime three times, so I yelled, "Grandma, what time is it?"

"You a nice-a boy," she called back.

What kind of answer is that? I wondered. It didn't occur to me that she had no need to know what time it was, and anyway she was probably as confused by that stupid clock as I was. (I guess that timepiece was just a comforting sound.)

After I entered the first grade, I didn't see her nearly so often, and a few years later her diabetes finally caught up with her and she passed away. Her wake was the first one I ever went to and to pass the time I snuck a penny into her casket on a dare from one of my cousins but I don't remember which one. A thousand years from now if archaeologists dig up her bones, I'll bet they'll never guess why that coin was buried with her.

Uncle Arnie

Things are not always what they first appear. Take my Uncle Arnie, for instance. When my dad was a young man of eighteen, Arnie was his best friend. They did everything together. They made money doing odd jobs, went on dates, even got into trouble together. My dad told the story of how he and Arnie were invited to a fancy formal dinner and after being seated, they were confronted with a maze of plates and cutlery the likes of which they had never seen before.

My father leaned toward Arnie and whispered, "There's a lemon in my water glass."

"So?" answered Arnie, "just drink it and shut up. Don't act like a rube."

As the first course was being cleared and Arnie and Dad's water glasses were now half full, they saw everyone else cleaning their fingers off in what they now knew were *finger bowls*.

"If they're trying to get the lemon out," Arnie said to my dad, "Someone should tell them that it's easier if you drink the water first."

They both began laughing so hard that they had to leave the table. They were still laughing about it twenty-five years later.

When my father was dating my mother, Arnie was dating her sister, Bea. They double dated and eventually both couples got married. As World War II approached, Arnie got a job at the South Boston Navy Yard and my dad at the Watertown Arsenal. My dad bought a house on Main Street in Winthrop; and Arnie and Bea had the apartment on the top floor while we lived on the second floor. They had to walk through our front hall to enter their flat. Arnie and Bea had a daughter, Patty, who was two weeks older than me (and she never let me forget it.)

Patty could run faster than me, was taller than me, and knew the facts of life before I did.

"Girls live inside their mothers for nine months before they're born," she told me, "Boys don't. So I'm much older than you!"

One December she changed my life, when during a discussion

concerning what we might get for Christmas, she said, "Don't tell me you still believe in Santa Claus! The next thing you'll tell me, is you think there's an Easter Bunny."

I was speechless, as I was pushed, against my will, out of childhood.

Aunt Bea was one of my favorites. She's the only family member who ever attended one of my little league baseball games. When Bobby Cox hit me on the head with a rock, causing me to bleed profusely, I went crying to my mother, who took one look at me and ran out of the house! I went upstairs and Aunt Bea comforted me until Doctor Costanza came and stitched me up.

Uncle Arnie always told good stories and built interesting things, like the first electric razor I ever heard of. It was the size of a small loaf of bread, built on thin plywood and sounded like a truck but to my amazement he shaved with it.

He took his coffee black and always carefully added precisely three grains of sugar, which he never stirred. As he drank the last bit of coffee he would show me the three grains of sugar on the bottom of the cup.

"I don't like it too sweet," he would tell me.

He read mysteries and liked to tell me how he knew who the murderer was before it was revealed in the book.

Because they entered their apartment through our front hallway (next to my room) I could hear Uncle Arnie coming up the stairs, carrying his empty lunch-pail in the evenings. Some nights he apparently worked late and kept to himself as he slowly walked up, mumbling and humming a tune. He didn't seem to notice me.

You might forgive a ten year old for not realizing that he was getting a glimpse of what was his darker side..

Occasionally I was told to be very quiet and not to bother them upstairs, especially on weekends.

Aunt Bea was a few years older than my mother, of slight build and had some health problems. For one thing, she often had blackened eyes.

"What's the matter with Aunt Bea's eyes?" I asked my mom.

"Oh, She needs to rest. The doctor gave her some pills," she replied.

One night my parents were arguing. Something about the rent

from upstairs.

"It's not her fault that he's that way," I heard my mother say.

The next day I asked, "Mom, is Aunt Bea okay? Why is her face all red?"

"She fell," I was told.

We visited upstairs less and less and when I was twelve, we moved to a new house. Uncle Arnie and Aunt Bea stopped being a part of my life. As I got older, I felt bad that I ever enjoyed his stories and hadn't seen through him. I don't know what people did to try and help Aunt Bea but I suspect, not enough. Of course, I was only ten years old and I might have gotten it all wrong... but I don't think so. It was 1956 and in 1956, if your husband came home drunk and beat you, you were on your own and out of luck.

I wonder if things have changed much.

The Beard

"Are you growing a beard?" Professor Kahn said as I walked by.

I heard him, but thought, *He couldn't be talking to me*, so I kept walking out of the classroom at the BU School of Education. That was May, 1967 and growing a beard wasn't anything I had ever even considered.

"Ernest, are you okay?" he called after me, "You don't look well."

"Oh, sorry Doctor Kahn. I've... I've had the flu {cough} and been in bed all week. I only got up to take the final and now I'm going home and back to bed {cough}."

"Well, that explains it," he said, "I hope you feel better. Oh, and shave when you get a chance. It wouldn't be much of a beard anyway."

An hour later, I was standing in front of the bathroom mirror in my Commonwealth Avenue apartment. I hadn't shaved for four days and there was definitely something noticeable on my face.

Hmm... I thought, *a beard... Might be cool.*

When Donna came home from work, I met her at the door.

"How would I look with a beard?"

"I think you'd look great," she said enthusiastically.

Donna and me (1968)

I had graduated MIT in January and after working briefly as an engineer at the Sensory Aid Center on campus I decided that if I was going to save the world I would do it as a teacher. There were only a few courses required to teach in Massachusetts so I signed up at the BU School of Education. It wasn't as challenging as my MIT days but I stuck with it. (In the Methods of Education course, we spent a whole class learning how to alphabetize a class-book! *Honest.*)

I saw an ad in the Globe for a teaching position at the Shaw Prep School on Boylston Street; only beginning it's second year. I had an interview and in September I began teaching math and science to a hundred fifty students who, for one reason or another, couldn't (or wouldn't) make it in a traditional public school.

The country was getting more and more polarized by the Vietnam War, by the length of your hair, by how you dressed and even by whether or not you had a beard. At this point, my beard was four months old and beginning to look like it belonged on my face. I thought it made me look older and at only 23 years old, every little bit helped. (Some of my students were only five years younger than me.)

My beard was very red then and occasionally brought me attention.

"Hey Red," a man outside the Copley Hotel called to me while I was chaperoning a school dance, "I'll give you fifty bucks if you shave off your beard."

I didn't hesitate.

At the time I only made $110 a week and I could grow the beard back for free, so I said, "Sure. There's a barber in the lobby," and began to walk there.

The man immediately withdrew the offer.

In France in 1968 there was serious domestic unrest and the government was almost overthrown. One of the leaders of the near revolution was a young man with a red beard (nicknamed 'Erik the Red' by the press) and he was on the loose. Donna and I were driving across France and we were pulled over by the Gendarmerie Nationale. When it was obvious that I was 'Ernie the Red' and not 'Erik the Red' they decided maybe they should take my rental car apart anyway, just in case. So they took the seats out, the rugs up, and emptied the trunk and the ashtrays. The interior of the car was strewn along the side of a pretty French country road.

"You may go," one of the policeman said to me as he walked back toward his car.

"Wait... wait," Donna and I both said, "you can't leave the car like this!"

They conferred, put the seats back in, then one of the policemen said, "Now... you may go."

Better than nothing, I thought as I put the rest of the car back together, *But maybe Erik the Red has the right idea.*

Here are a few beard facts and observations:

- A lot of hippies had grown beards, so at anti-war rallies in the sixties, there were a lot of beards about. While young demonstrators chanted, "Hell no, we won't go!" some people taunted us. "Hippie commie freaks!" they shouted. It seemed that all the taunters were clean shaven. But it didn't really matter if you had facial hair or not; nobody listened to anybody.
- Fidel Castro had a beard. He appeared to be a hero to the downtrodden in Cuba but by 1967 it was pretty obvious to me that Fidel was in over his head. And he was definitely giving beards a bad name.
- The last President of the United States with a beard was Benjamin Harrison in 1893. Hardly anyone has ever even heard of him. (*Wasn't he was one of the Beatles?*)
- An American (King C. Gillette) invented the double edge safety razor, so it seemed un-American to not shave.
- Donna's grandmother thought my beard made me look like an animal. I suppose that could have been meant as a compliment... but I don't think it was.
- My mother loved me so unconditionally, she probably didn't even notice I had a beard.

Benjamin Harrison

- Donna likes my beard.
- Babies invariably pull it (and that can hurt).
- Since it turned white, I've been mistaken for Santa Claus a number of times.

One January day while I was walking along, a little four year old came running toward me, followed close behind by his mother trying to keep up. He was holding something in his hand and as he approached me, he held it up for me to see. It was a toy truck. "Very nice," I said.

His mother finally arrived and although out of breath still managed to say, "You gave it to him... Santa."

I looked down at him, smiled and said, "If you're good, there will be many more like it."

- Another time a little girl looked at me and asked her mother, "Is that the real Santa?"

Her mother said, "I think so. Go ask him."

The little girl approached me and said, "Santa, are you going to give me the X-box I asked you for?"

A terrified look came over the mother's face and she flashed me the cut sign.

"Have you been good," I asked and the little girl answered "Yes."

The mother frantically mouthed, *"No! No!"* my way.

"Since you've been so good," I said, "I think there's a good chance you will get it."

If a mother's look could kill... I'd be dead.
- None of my children have ever seen me without a beard.
- I forget I have a beard until I'm near a mirror but it always keeps my face warm in winter anyway.
- It has saved me a lot of time preparing to go out, through the years. If you spend three minutes a day shaving, in forty years that's 360 hours or fifteen days. Couldn't you find a better use of fifteen days?
- My father hated my beard so much that he wouldn't be seen in public with me. He eventually learned to live with it.
- When my sister was a baby, my father maintained lighthouses with the Coast Guard. He got stranded on a Boston Harbor Island for three days during a hurricane and when he finally came home he had a small beard. My sister wouldn't go near him until he shaved it off.
- My beard covers a cleft in my chin that Donna (at least while we were dating) said, "was cute."
- When I was twelve, my Aunt Virginia, who was half Navajo Indian, told me that her brother couldn't grow a beard. "No Navajos can" she told me. We didn't have Google then, so I

couldn't find out if it was true. *(It is.)*
- I can only think of two things that a man *can* do, that a woman *can't*. One is pee accurately while standing up and the other is grow a beard. Unfortunately for men, neither is very important these days.

Kids

The First:

The weather was mild enough for Donna and I to drive to the 1969 Cataldo Family Christmas Party on my motorcycle. The place was full of aunts, uncles and cousins. There was music and lasagna and wine. My father was filming the festivities in the catered hall somewhere in East Boston, using his 8 mm movie camera with the flood-light attachment. These events were barely tolerable even without someone following you around saying, "Smile, look at the camera and do something."

Donna and I decided to use the occasion to tell everyone that, after being married for four years, we were going to have a baby. First we approached my mother. Donna stood proudly as if it would be possible to discern anything about her condition, in the second month, while she was wearing a Christmas sweater.

"Mom, Donna is pregnant," I said.

My mother let out a little shriek, excitedly wrapped her arms around me and exclaimed, "I knew you could do it!"

"Wow," I said to Donna over my shoulder, "I guess people were worried that we couldn't figure it out."

As the summer of 1970 approached, Donna and I were living in-- and still renovating-- our new house on Beacon Hill and were getting around on my Yamaha motorcycle as we waited for the birth. It wasn't usual (or easy) then to find out the sex of a baby before the delivery, so we had to have two names ready. I read that Ringo Starr had a baby named Zak.

"How about Zac with a 'C'," I said, "If his middle name starts with an A, then his initials will be his first name."

"What if is it's a girl?" Donna asked. After a moment she said, "How about Apple?"

"Apple Cataldo?" I said, "I don't know..."

It had better be a boy, I thought, *although if her middle name were Betty, her initials...*

The due date was June 25th but it wasn't until a hot Sunday afternoon in early August that we had to rush to the hospital.

My motorcycle had been stolen a couple of weeks before so we cabbed through the traffic created by a Red Sox game at Fenway Park, and arrived at the hospital just to be told, "Go home. It's not time yet."

A half hour later we arrived back home and Donna said, "It's time. I'm certain of it!"

So we got back in a cab and after maneuvering through the same traffic we were in the delivery room. There were triplets being delivered in the room across the hall, taking up all the available nurses, so I was told I might be needed, as more than an observer, at the birth.

Donna was squeezing my hand and pushing as hard as she could. The doctor was poised at the end of the table while off in the distance we could just make out a woman screaming, *"I'm not pushing anymore!"*

Three day old Zac (1970)

A nurse came in and said quietly, "One more to go over there."

It didn't appear that Donna heard any of this; she was too busy pushing.

The doctor looked up at me and asked, "Who won the Red Sox game today?"

While I tried to remember, he looked down and shouted, "Here it comes!"

And a baby appeared.

"It's a boy," I said, "It's Zac!"

Thank God..., I thought, *No Apple.*

He was red, wet, wrinkled and had a birth mark on his forehead. Everyone commented on how beautiful he was.

Later while Donna was holding him and nursing, it occurred to me that the baby was entirely, totally, completely dependent on us. No screw-ups allowed for the next eighteen years! It was frightening; but I eventually came to grips with it. And in time, Zac and I enjoyed watching Sesame Street together on Saturday mornings, while he lay across my stomach.

The Second:

"Is this Mr. Cataldo," the voice on the phone asked.

"Yes," I answered.

"This is the Holt Adoption Agency in Seattle... Good news. We have a child for you. A five week old girl in Seoul, Korea."

"That's great," I said, "When--"

"We sent a photograph to your social worker and we'd like you to look at the picture and decide."

"Decide what?" I asked, "Does she have two heads?"

"Why... no," she said; a little taken aback.

"Then we'll take her'" I said emphatically, "Sign us up. When will it happen?"

"We're only awaiting the paperwork from the State Department," she said.

That was in April of 1974.

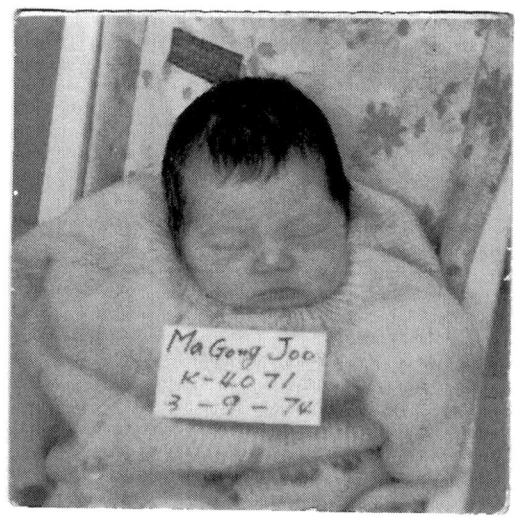

Kouri in Seoul (1974)

Two months and twenty phone calls later, Donna and I were at our wits end. We tried calling Senator Ted Kennedy's office. They were sympathetic but no help.

"Mr. Cataldo, you see... the State Department is part of the executive branch and they resent interference from ..."

Now we were frantic. I called Flip (who at the time was a legislative aide to Congressman Drinan in Washington) and re-told the saga. He and Toddy had adopted a Korean girl six months previous, so he was doubly sympathetic.

"I have a friend in the State Department who owes me a favor," he said, "I'll see what I can do."

He called me back that evening and assured me, "They're working on it."

The following morning the phone rang. It was the Holt Adoption Agency.

"She's on her way," a woman's voice said, "You can pick her up tomorrow at JFK airport in New York."

We found out a few days later that Flip's friend got his boss at the State Department to send a telegram to the embassy in Seoul, telling them to *send the baby or explain the delay*. His boss was Henry Kissinger, the then Secretary of State. (If the baby had been a boy we might have named him Henry.)

We borrowed my father's car, drove to New York and watched as the Boeing 747 was emptied of regular passengers. Most remained at the gate to watch the children from Korea being united with their new adopted families. A woman carried a baby wearing a yellow dress embossed with the word "Holt" on a sleeve over to us. She was called Ma Gong Joo at the orphanage but after some research we discovered a Korean folk tale with a girl named Kou-Ri. What a great moment as Donna, Zac and I met, the now four month old, Kouri Mia Cataldo for the first time.

On the ride home, Zac, soon to be four years old, said, "Well, I guess I'm not the cutest anymore."

He was right.

The grandparents were supportive, with varying degrees of enthusiasm. Mimi especially was overjoyed to have another little one in the family. My mother and father were welcoming and Donna's father was tolerant.

After six months, the adoption became final but we had to wait three years to petition for Kouri to gain U.S. Citizenship. Finally we were in the INS (now called ICE) Office at Government Center. Kouri sat with a coloring book on the floor while Donna and I spoke with an immigration officer. He read over her form then asked a few questions.

"Has she ever belonged to a group that advocates the violent overthrow of the government?" he asked.

Donna and I looked at each other, then at him.

"She's three years old," I said.

"I know," he replied, "but I'm required to ask these questions. I'm sorry. Feel free to answer for her."

"No," I answered for her.

He continued with the questions, "Does she subscribe to any magazines that advocate the violent overthrow of the government?"

"She's three years old," I said, "She can't read."

"Please answer the question," he pleaded, clearly embarrassed.

"No," I answered for her.

There were a few more similar questions, then my mother and father, as her sponsors were interviewed and in a few weeks we were before a judge, reciting an oath for Kouri as she (and a hundred other applicants) became an American citizen. It was a day that I was especially proud to be an American.

People asked if we thought having a child of a different race would be difficult.

"I don't know but we'll find out," I said.

I think the question is best answered by a scene at Winthrop Beach when Kouri was four and sitting on the sand with her grandmother, Mimi.

A little Asian boy was playing a short distance away and Mimi said, "Kouri, that little boy over there may be Korean. Why don't you go say hello to him."

"Oh, Mimi," Kouri replied, "He's Chinese."

Mimi was very impressed and assumed Kouri, being Korean herself, had some way of knowing such things, so she said, "That's remarkable. How do you know that?"

Kouri put down her plastic shovel, looked at Mimi and said, "I've been to Chinese restaurants."

The Third:

"Is this Mr. Cataldo," the voice on the phone asked.

"Yes," I answered.

"This is the Massachusetts Department of Children Services... We've heard from Texas Catholic Charities and they have a child for you. A five week old girl in Amarillo."

"That's great," I said, "When--"

"We have a picture here at the office and we'd like you to look at it and decide."

"I don't think we need to look at the picture--"

"She's black," she interrupted.

Chloe in Texas (1978)

After absorbing what she said, I replied, "That doesn't matter... unless it would be better to place her with a black family."

"They've tried and had no luck. Getting her into a family while she's an infant is their top priority."

"Then she's in ours," I said, "When is she coming?"

Zac, who had been hoping for a brother this time, was a little disappointed when he found out it was another girl. Then I called my father to tell him the news.

"Dad, we've adopted another baby. A five week old girl... "

"Oh?" he said. Not sure what might be coming next.

"...and she's black," I said.

"There was a slight pause, then he asked, "Is she Korean too?"

"No," I replied, "Texan."

"Well ... congratulations," he said.

Zac, Kouri, Donna and I met Chloe at Logan Airport. She was incredibly cute and tiny and quiet. Too quiet we thought. We brought her to the doctor right away.

"She's not responding to noises," he said, "Probably the flight has temporarily affected her hearing and she may not have gotten much stimulation until now." He stretched her out on the examining table and said, "And let's fatten her up a bit."

We did our best and she was soon responding to, and making plenty of her own, noise.

Once more, the grandparents were wonderful and supportive, especially Mimi and once more the questions arose about a multiracial family.

One day arriving home from first grade, Chloe showed me her homework assignment which was to color in a picture of Martin Luther King, Jr. We told her what a great man he had been and how it was about time he had a holiday named after him.

"You better get that done before supper," I suggested.

She headed up the stairs, then stopped half way and faced me.

"What color is he?" she called down.

"Use the brown crayon," I replied, " he's like you."

It's hard to imagine a little black girl having a whiter father, and Chloe did ask me to not tell people who I was when I visited her elementary school, but actually, I would have said the same thing to my father (if he ever came to my school, which he didn't.)

We did our best and despite some minor bumps we managed and I couldn't imagine three better kids. I'm not sure if all the aunts, uncles and cousins knew what to make of us but (at least publicly) all were positive.

Six years later we were driving to Quebec.

As we crossed into Canada, a border guard looked into our van, eyed Zac, Kouri, Chloe, Donna and I, and said, "What is this? Some kind of school trip?"

"No...," I replied proudly, "It's my family."

The Secret

Warren and I had a secret. I didn't have to worry that he would divulge it, because he couldn't talk. He was only eight months old.

His mother, my Aunt Kay, had contracted polio and was confined to a mechanical breathing device, called an iron lung, to keep her alive. His father, my Uncle Jimmy, was a stone mason and between his job and the time he spent at the race track, was unable to care for the boy, so my mom and dad took Warren in. A crib was set up in what was our TV area, adjacent to my room and in the summer of 1950, I suddenly had a 'younger brother'. I liked having him around to play with. He didn't object to being the Indian to my cowboy or the monster that my electric train was racing to avoid. My parents and older sister did all the hard stuff, although I occasionally fed him a kind of rice cereal.

"Warren, open up... here it comes... one for you... and one for me..."

I really liked the stuff more than he did, and even ate it when no one was around to see me.

Whenever Warren fussed at night, I was the first to hear him and I would retrieve a cup from under my bed, tip-toe out of my room and up to his crib.

"Hey Warren," I whispered as I showed him the empty cup, "Shhh... just wait here. I'll be right back."

He knew what was coming, so he sat quietly and watched me sneak down the hall, past my parent's room and into the kitchen. The refrigerator was the hard part; the latch was noisy and I was sure the light would give me away. So I unplugged the refrigerator first and ever so slo-w-ly pulled on the handle to release the catch, took out the bottle, poured some in the cup, put the bottle back and then ever so slo-w-ly pushed the door closed while holding the handle out. Then I re-plugged the refrigerator. Considering this all took place in virtual darkness, it was remarkable that in less than a minute I returned to the crib carrying the small metal sipping cup.

"Here it is," I assured Warren as he reached through the side of the crib and pulled the cup to his lips, "Take it easy. Make it last.

How much Coca-Cola do you think we have?" I whispered.

He made no attempt to make it last and when the cup was quickly emptied, he settled down. Then despite it being summer, I softly sang him a Christmas song, because the only songs I knew were Christmas songs.

Then I said, "Nighty-night," took the cup into my room and re-hid it under my bed. Finally we both went back to sleep and our secret was safe for one more day.

When my parents told everyone that I was the only one in the house that could quiet the baby down when he was crying, Warren and I would lock eyes and we knew what the other was thinking,

"Don't worry, the secret's safe with me, bro."

The King and I

Picture if you can, a time when there were no cell phones, no internet and especially no ATM machines. Banks opened no earlier than 9:00 AM and closed whenever they damn well pleased; often before 3:00 PM and the idea of a bank being open on a Saturday or Sunday was unimaginable. Unless you were unemployed (and therefore, probably had little need of a bank) a bank transaction took considerable advanced planning. Lunchtime was an obvious choice for me, except of course I wasn't the only one thinking that way, so even when I arrived a little before noon, the lines were long.

Once in a line it was just a matter of daydreaming, shuffling along, following the person in front of you and waiting for the magic word, "Next!".

So it was on a Spring day in 1976 as I entered the State Street Bank in Government Center just before noon. I passed a bronze plaque alluding to the possibility that President George Washington had slept in a building that occupied this spot in 1792. I stepped past the faux marble columns and into the busy main concourse where I looked over the situation. All twenty stations in this main branch were open but engaged, so I settled on Mrs. Peterson's line. She had worked in the branch since just after Washington slept there and she knew her way around any bank transaction. And the displayed pictures of her many grandchildren added a nice touch. I occasionally brought the kids along and she always made a fuss about them (to the dismay of the people behind me in line.)

Today there were only five people in front of me, but the lunchtime crowd had just arrived and filled in behind.

As the line slowly advanced, the tall, distinguished, impeccably dressed and coiffed gentleman standing in front of me, turned to face me.

Oh-oh, I hope he's not going to ask me to hold his place, I thought. I could almost hear the grumbling starting behind me.

"Excuse me young man but could you help me?" he said in perfect English but with a very distinct Spanish accent.

Foreign businessman, I thought.

"Certainly," I answered, "if I can."

He held up a partially filled-out withdrawal slip while holding a foreign passport in his other hand and said, "Could you tell me what I should write in this space... to withdraw from my account?"

He pointed to the line in question with a free finger while keeping the *amount* box covered with his thumb.

"That's where you would put-- what we call-- a ZIP code," I explained, "but I think you just leave it blank if your address is not in the States."

"Yes, I am here in Boston only for a few days," he said, "and thank you so much for your assistance."

He slid the withdrawal slip into his passport then reached in his coat pocket, pulled out a leather wallet and handed me a business card. "Have you ever been to Spain?" he asked.

"Yes, on my honeymoon," I said, "and we loved it."

"Wonderful," he said, "and if you come again, I would be pleased if you would stop and see me."

I nodded and I swear he clicked his heels together before turning to face the front of the line again. A moment later he was called to the window so I looked down at the card that he had just given me.

It read: ***Juan Carlos, King of Spain - Palacio de la Zarzuela, Madrid***

I stared at him standing at the window talking to Mrs. Peterson.

He thinks he's the King of Spain I thought and chuckled for a second. But something made me stop and begin furtively glancing around the room.

If he's a king, he's got to have bodyguards, I said to myself.

They weren't obvious at first but as he finished and walked toward the door, two men, dressed in similar blazers got in step and walked with him.

"NEXT!" Mrs. Peterson called out.

I stepped up to the window.

"Good morning," she said, "and how are your children today?"

"Oh, fine," I said while looking to see if the three men had exited the building. Then I asked, "Do you know who that was?"

I showed her the card.

"Oh my! Do you think it's true?" she said, "His passport did say

Spain."

"I don't know. It doesn't seem likely, does it" I said.

"Wait 'til Ellie hears about this!"

"Ellie?"

"My granddaughter. She's eleven you know and learning the world capitals," she said and glanced at the framed picture sitting next to her.

Someone behind me in the line cleared his throat a little louder than was necessary.

It occurred to me that Mrs. Peterson and I could get to the bottom this if she would let me take a look at that withdrawal slip (had he taken the money in gold doubloons?) but then thought better of it. I made my bank deposit and stepped away.

"Bring the children next time," she told me then called out, "NEXT."

Back out on the sidewalk, nothing looked out of the ordinary. *King of Spain,* I said to myself, *no way!*

That night, at home, I showed Donna the card and looked through an old dusty reference encyclopedia trying to find a picture of the King of Spain but had to content myself with a likeness of the fascist dictator, Generalissimo Franco (who had just died a year before) and a painting of King Ferdinand talking with Christopher Columbus.

About twenty years later I came across that business card while cleaning my desk, so I sat down at my computer and typed in *Juan Carlos* on WebCrawler. An article with a picture slowly scanned onto the screen.

"Donna, come here! It's him! This was the guy at the bank! He is the King of Spain!"

The article said he had been put on the throne when Franco died in 1975 and had been in the United States many times including his honeymoon in 1962 and as king he visited the JFK library in Boston in... *June 1976!*

The cellphone had not yet been invented, so I don't have a selfie taken with him and I never did take him up on the offer to visit him at the palace but it certainly has increased my position in the six degrees of separation game (I assume kings hang around with other kings and heads of state and the like.)

By the way, the palace was not the Grand Palace of the old time kings but a more modest one of only 33,000 square feet in the outskirts of Madrid. Unfortunately, after a scandal involving the hunting of elephants in Botswana, he was deposed in 2014 and his son took over the throne.

So there you have it. I won't argue that an ATM machine isn't more convenient and quicker than the old bank tellers were (and open on weekends too) but if I had used an ATM machine back then, I would have likely never met an actual, honest to goodness king (or Mrs. Peterson for that matter.)

Baseball Memories

"Holy cow! Look at how *green* it is!" I shouted when I got my first glimpse of the field.

My thirteen year old cousin Tony beamed a big smile and said, "I told you you'd like it; didn't I?"

After a long involved bus, subway and trolley ride we had just walked up the passageway into Braves Field where I got my first glimpse inside of Boston's National League baseball park. I just couldn't get over how green it was.

"They must water this every day," I said above the din of the crowd.

"I'll bet they do," Tony replied.

The enormous, perfect green lawn was an amazing sight especially to someone who had to help cut the grass in his own small weed prone yard with a push lawnmower.

I was seven when Tony taught me to play baseball, took me to see my first major league game and showed me how to fill out a baseball scorecard. We went to doubleheaders on Sundays and stayed for both games. We saw Warren Spahn and Johnny Sain pitch. (The story goes that when about to face them both on a summer Sunday, opponents were heard to say, "Spahn and Sain, so pray for rain.) Eddie Matthews played third and I learned why you had to pay attention to every play when, while fiddling with my Crackerjacks box (looking for the prize) the crowd suddenly stood up and cheered wildly.

"What happened?" I asked Tony.

"Mathews started a triple play," he said, "You won't see another one of those this year."

I stood on my seat straining to see the Braves running into the dugout and congratulating Eddie. There was no replay back then so at best, I might see a grainy black and white still photograph the next day in the newspaper. To make matters worse, the Crackerjack prize was a dumb whistle thing that didn't even work.

I saw Sid Gordon hit a home run and watched enthralled as Sam 'Go-Go' Jethro stole a base. It was so wonderful, it seemed too good to be true... and of course... it was. The next year the Boston Braves announced that they were moving to Milwaukee.

"Now what do we do?" I whined.

"Don't worry, we can still go see the Red Sox," Tony said.

"The Red Sox? The American League... 19 games out of first place... Red Sox?... Those Red Sox?" I asked.

Even with Ted Williams, the Red Sox weren't much to cheer about back then, but with no other choice available they became my home team. It was hard to believe, but the *wait 'til next year* Red Sox were my home team. It was all we had, so we made the best of it and waited.

...

The older kids in my neighborhood played a pick-up baseball game every summer evening at Miller's athletic field until it got dark. Luckily my family ate supper early (Dad wanted food on the table when he got home from work) so I could rush through my part of the clean-up (I wiped the dishes dry) and head out the door before six.

"You be back in this house when the street lights come on," my mother ordered as I left, "or else your father will see that-- "

I was on the porch and on my way to the field by the time the threat was half finished. I showed up at Miller's Field every night on time and wanted to play in the worst way but being so young, I was never chosen. Instead, I sat behind the chain link fence along the first base line holding my glove and watched. The games were rarely close affairs and usually ended without much fuss when it got too dark to play but this one night, after a hard-played five innings, the score was close and the game was on the line as the street lights began flickering on.

Suddenly without warning, the first baseman stood up straight and called out, "Jeez, I gotta get home!"

He abandoned his position and ran off.

"Hey, Don't go! Just one more out," the pitcher yelled, "We're gonna win this thing!"

But the former first baseman just kept going. The rest of the defense tentatively held their ground as the pitcher looked around. Then he spotted me.

"Hey kid," he shouted, "Yes, you! Can you catch?"
I stood up, with my glove on and yelled, "Sure."
"Get at first base. Hurry up!" he said and then turned to face home plate.
I ran to my post, and hardly had two seconds to get set when the batter swung.
It was a foul pop-up, not very high, along the first base fence where I had just been sitting. I ran toward it, leaned into the fence, reached up and... caught it!
"We win, suckers!" yelled the pitcher as everyone ran off the field to get home, now that the street lights were on.
After the catch, I savored the moment and stood, ball in glove, leaning against the fence as one of my new teammates (and new friend?) ran toward me.
"What are ya' doing; posing for animal crackers?" he asked as he held his hand out, palm up. "That's my ball. Give it here!"
Okay... so they didn't carry me off the field on their shoulders, but I *had* caught the ball and I didn't even care that I was going to be really late getting home. I did get yelled at but it was a small price to pay, because the very next evening (after promising my parents to never be late again) I was picked to play. Yes, I was the *last* chosen... but I was picked... and I played. And I played every evening from then on.
The next summer my friends and I cleared a vacant lot near my house on Banks Street across from the army base. We cut weeds and raked dirt and removed rocks until it was just barely usable, but it was ours and we could play any time we wanted to. But there were two downsides. The first problem was that automobiles drove through the outfield. When an outfielder spotted a car coming along Banks Street he simply yelled, "Time out-- car coming!" This either halted play for a few seconds, until the car passed, or produced a huge argument about whether time-out had been called before or after a play had commenced. There were never any fatalities although I think Bobby Raitman broke a tooth on a fire hydrant, getting out of the way of a car once. Secondly, when someone hit a home run, the ball disappeared over the eight foot high, barb-wire topped, chain-link fence around the army base. Considerable athletic prowess was required to get over the barbed

wire without injury. Once over, you were prodded and cajoled to throw the ball back onto the playing field but only a novice would fall for that. If you threw the ball back, play continued without you while you were risking your life getting over the barbed wire again; all the while yelling, "Hey! Wait up."

You quickly learned to stick the ball in your pocket while you climbed back over the fence and let them wait.

By 1956, my friends and I would collect a bunch of empty soda bottles that our neighbors left on their back porches, return them to Bandy's Drug Store for the deposit then take the bus and subway to Fenway Park. It involved changing trains at Scollay Square where we would spend some time running up the *down* escalator (and vice-a-versa) until our train to Kenmore Square came in. At the park, there was no way we could afford the grandstand at $1.70 so we opted for a bleacher unreserved bench seat for 35 cents. But mid-week, day games drew a very small crowd (a few thousand people) so we waited until the third inning when the attendant at the gate separating the bleachers from the rest of the park got so bored that he would wander from his post long enough for the four of us to run by. With 30,000 empty seats to choose from, we should have had no trouble disappearing into the vast stadium, but we were usually not satisfied with the grandstand where we might have remained unnoticed. Instead we headed for the totally barren box seats down by the field. Within minutes an elderly employee wearing a red jacket confronted us.

"May I see your tickets please," he said knowingly.

"Our other friend has them... and he's... "

At this point half of us said, " ...getting a hot dog," while the other half replied, " ...gone to the men's room."

The man in the red jacket appeared skeptical.

"Well, you go sit up in the grandstand until he returns," he said and pointed the way.

This scene repeated itself four or five times over the course of the next few innings.

We would pick up a program that someone had discarded and fill out a scorecard for an inning or two for no reason other than that we could. A boiled hot dog and a Coke was twenty-five cents and a box of Crackerjacks; a dime. (The prize inside the box was often more interesting than the game.)

    We paid attention when Ted Williams got up (we seemed to know we were watching greatness) or a fly ball was hit near Jimmy Pearsall (you never knew what craziness was forthcoming) and after the game (likely a Red Sox loss) there would be another round of up the *down* escalator (and vice-a-versa) at Scolley Square before I made it home late to five o'clock supper.

    Over the next decade, the Red Sox only got worse which at least made it very easy to walk from my college fraternity to Fenway Park on a warm Friday evening in the Spring and get good seats. The year I got married, the Red Sox came in last in the American league, twenty-six games out.

. . .

    When I was old enough to play in the little league, the coach decided I should be a pitcher. The Red Sox were so pathetic that my favorite pitcher at the time was a Yankee; Whitey Ford. He was left handed and great. I was right handed and awful. But we were both nicknamed, Whitey. My pitching career was short-lived and I ended up playing mostly in the infield.

    Forty years later, I was visiting my parents at their Ft. Lauderdale condo when I stepped into the elevator with my Dad. There was Whitey Ford! Our eyes met for just a second. He was shorter than I thought he should be.

    "Do you know who that is?" my father quizzed me, not trying to be discrete.

    "Yes," I whispered uncomfortably.

    "Who is it then?" my father challenged in a loud voice.

    I'm not sure who was more embarrassed, Whitey or me.

    "It's Whitey Ford." I said quietly as the great former pitcher nodded his head toward me.

    "You recognized him from the Wheaties box, did ya?" Dad said.

    "Yeah," I answered softly, "the Wheaties box."

    Mercifully the doors parted and Whitey smiled as he stepped out onto his floor.

    The doors closed and dad said, "Was he pretty good?"

    "Well he made it onto the Wheaties Box, didn't he?" I said.

...

In 1967, Flip knocked on my door and asked, "You want to go to the Red Sox home opener tomorrow? They finished in last place last year so tickets should be easy to get."

The next day at one, we walked the twenty minutes to Fenway Park and purchased bleacher seats, but the chain-link fence at the entrance remained closed until fifteen minutes before the game. It was a young boisterous crowd so when the gate opened there was a rush of bodies to squeeze through the five foot opening.

It was scary; so after the game, walking home Flip said, "Next year let's get tickets in advance in the grandstand."

That was fifty plus years ago and we're still going. The group grew to eight and for a few years we watched from a luxury box. Now there are three generations attending! We've had games rained out, snowed out and frozen out but there are very few things I look forward to more than Red Sox opening day.

In 2003, for the first time since my father was five years old, the Red Sox were on the verge of finally winning it all; but Grady Little, their pin-head manager, left the pitcher in a game too long and they lost to the Yankees. Driving on the turnpike the next morning, I saw a bedsheet that was hastily hung from an overpass on which was scrawled, KILL GRADY LITTLE. I didn't know where he was hiding, so I couldn't.

In 2004, they got it all together and after falling behind three games to none to the Yankees, went on to win eight games in a row and the World Series! (Thank you Doug Roberts.)

To best explain how I felt after the comeback and subsequent World Series win, I'll simply paraphrase Mrs. Miller, "Oh Lord, you can take me now if you want."

And speaking of the Lord taking; when my uncle Freddy (one of dad's step-brothers) was dying, my dad went to be with him. Lying in his bed, Freddie held up a baseball.

"Give this to Ernie," he said, "I know he likes baseball; he'll enjoy it."

Freddie had a restaurant in downtown Boston, and when major league teams were in town, he would comp drinks to the players if they would autograph the baseballs that he kept under the bar. The ball he gave me was a 1961 Yankees team ball. Mickey Mantle, Roger Maris, Yogi Berra, Whitey Ford... the whole team. What a piece of baseball history. I was offered $2500 for it soon after but to me, it was priceless. I hope whoever stole it from my house ten years later enjoys it (and then chokes on it.)

Wedding Gifts

The last thing I expected as we exited the shuttle flight from New York was to see my parents waiting for us. We had just endured a grueling sixteen hour flight from London to New York (after one engine quit over the Atlantic) and wanted nothing more than a place to lie down. Except for a brief phone call from Copenhagen requesting money, we had had no contact with anyone in the family for the three months of our honeymoon and we had perhaps forgotten our lowly position in that hierarchy.

I put down the duffle bag that had contained everything we owned since our wedding day and hugged my mother. Then my dad stepped forward and deflected an attempted hug with a quarter turn and an extended hand.

"How was it?" he asked.

"It was great! We had--"

He wasn't listening but put his mouth next to my ear and said, "If anybody asks, you had $15,000 in the safe at my house."

I stepped back so I could look at him and managed to say, "What?... Who would ask?"

"The State Police or the IRS," he replied as if that cleared things up.

"$15,000 at your house?... Why would I have... How could I have that kind of money at your house? Where would I get $15,000?"

(For reference, $15,000 in 1966 was the equivalent of $120,000 now.)

"Wedding presents," he said.

"Wedding presents!" I repeated too loudly for my dad's liking. He tried to continue, "If the FBI asks you--"

I threw up my hands.

FBI? IRS? What is going on? I thought.

He motioned me to a quiet spot near the windows in the terminal, where on a different day I might have watched the planes taxiing to and from the gates, and said, "Listen; thieves broke in the house and robbed my wall safe. I called the police and reported it without thinking and now the IRS wants to know how I came to have that much cash in my house... so I told them it was from your wedding and I was holding it for you until you got home."

As great as my honeymoon had been, traveling four thousand miles around Europe on a motorcycle and visiting fabulous places, I had actually been looking forward to coming home, finishing school, getting an apartment and starting my domestic life. Now I wasn't so sure.

"Dad, I don't think I could pull that off. You of all people should know that I'm not a very good liar and--"

A disgusted look appeared on his face and he said, "You're just like your mother."

"How did they get the safe open?" I asked trying to deflect the conversation away from my obvious failings.

"They took the whole wall," he replied, "cut through the plaster and the studs and took the wall."

The last few years dad had taken to hanging around with 'associates' of Uncle Sal and I suspect they had no trouble figuring out where the safe that dad talked about constantly was located.

We left Logan Airport and on the ride back to Winthrop I asked, "Did they steal anything else?"

"Yes," Dad said, "your watch."

"Watch? What watch?"

"The one you've been talking about for the past year. The one you wanted. The one your mother and I got you as a wedding present," he said.

"Oh."

At that moment, I wished I was less like my mother and a better liar.

But even without my help dad got through that incident okay (likely with much advice from Uncle Sal) and was audited by the IRS every year thereafter. Fortunately for all concerned, they never questioned me about it.

We, of course, got many gifts from our family (my father-in-law, you may recall, wired half of five hundred dollars to us in Copenhagen) and the almost four hundred guests our parents had invited to the wedding, mostly money but with a few typical wedding presents in the mix: vases, towels, electric coffee pots and the like.

Just before we left the reception, my fraternity brother and best college friend, Bill Morton walked up to us, kissed Donna (he always liked Donna), shook my hand, wished me luck and held out a book of matches.

"Here," he said, "These might come in handy."

He had quite the sense of humor and was always quick with a joke, so I thanked him and put the matches in my pocket. Donna and I said our good-byes and caught a taxi to the airport. In the cab I took out the matchbook, looking for what deeper gag might lie within. Nothing obvious outside, but when I open the cover, out fell a carefully folded fifty dollar bill! As far as I'm concerned, it was the best wedding gift we got. Not only was it a lot of money back then, but it really did come in handy. I had twenty dollars left in my wallet when we landed back in the States... so without the matchbook I would have been thirty dollars short!

Wedding reception- Bill Morton on right

And finally, even though I didn't smoke or go camping, the book of matches came in handy one more time. We had a wobbly table in a Paris cafe one night so I put it under one of the legs to steady it.

Who knows, maybe it's still there.

CSI Beacon Hill

I was sitting in my first floor, front room office on a warm summer afternoon when a couple walked by the open window.

A young man whispered, *"That's where the moped was when I grabbed it."*

I sat up straight in my chair and peered out at the sidewalk to see a young couple side by side. I decided to follow them.

A week earlier my son Zac's moped had disappeared from behind our house. We reported it stolen to the police, they came and filled out a report but didn't offer us much hope of finding it.

"Do you have any idea who took it," they asked.

"No, but we did find this expired Massachusetts driver learner's permit on the ground near where the bike had been," we told them.

It had gotten wet and the ink had run but you could still make out an address on Anderson Street, Boston. The policeman looked at it and handed it back to me with a look that said, *"What do you want me to do? Arrest him for littering?"*

The police left, I threw the evidence on my desk and Zac and I resigned ourselves to never seeing the moped again.

The couple I was following walked across Cambridge Street and into the Stop & Shop. I waited outside until twenty minutes later when they came out, each carrying a bag of groceries. I followed them back across Cambridge Street, up Garden and past my windows once more. Incredibly, they turned up Anderson Street. I was following at a safe distance, so I hurried to the corner to see what door they would go into. When I arrived and looked up the street, my heart sank... they had disappeared. Then I heard a basement door close and latch just one house up. I got closer and it was number 28-B Anderson Street.

What was the address on that permit? I wondered as I hurried back to my office.

I moved a week's worth of papers and bills around until I uncovered it.

28-B Anderson Street it read.

It only took a minute for me to come up with a plan.

I phoned the District A police station, gave my name, address and phone number, then asked, "Can I speak to the detective in charge of the stolen Phillips Street moped?"

"There's no detective on that case," the voice on the phone said condescendingly, "If it's less than $2000 it's not assigned to anyone."

"But I know who did it," I said.

"That's swell, but no one has the case. Sorry." <click>

I hung up and remained seated at my desk for a few minutes while the sun set and I pondered what to do next. Then the phone rang.

"This is Detective Sasso from District A. Tell me what you know about the stolen moped. You have twenty seconds."

I explained about the permit card, what I had heard at my window and about following the suspects.

"Wait there, I'll be right over," he said, and hung up.

My heart was pounding.

What have I done?, I thought when I heard a car horn beeping and then a commotion out in front of my house.

I looked out the window to see a man placing a revolving blue light on the roof of a Ford Crown Victoria that was stopped in the middle of Phillips Street.

"Back the fuck up! I'm parking here," the man yelled toward the beeping car behind him.

Ten seconds later my doorbell rang. A man in an ill-fitting suit was standing on my stoop with a uniformed officer standing behind him.

"I'm Detective Sasso," the man informed me, "Show me where they went."

The three of us walked around the corner and I pointed to the door of the basement apartment: 28-B Anderson Street.

"You're sure about this, right?" Detective Sasso asked me.

"Yes," I said.

Pretty sure, I thought to myself.

Detective Sasso pointed down the three steps toward the basement apartment door, looked at the uniformed officer and said, "Kick the door in!"

"What?" asked the officer.

Detective Sasso looked at me and said, "Move back, you don't want to see this." Then he turned again to the officer, "Kick the door in!"

The officer descended the three steps and kicked in the cheap, hollow core door, then stepped aside as a flashlight wielding Detective Sasso rushed it, shone the light in the young male occupant's face and shouted, "You can go to prison for two years for larceny of the motorcycle or you can tell me where the bike is and I'll walk out of here and leave you alone! Where is the bike?"

"Park's Garage in Waltham," the young man said immediately.

Detective Sasso walked up the steps, called me over and said, "I can't arrest him. This won't hold up in court you understand... but you get the bike back. Okay?"

I looked at the uniformed officer. He seemed as dumbfounded as I was.

"Okay," I said.

The next day I contacted Park's Garage and they told me I owed them a week's storage fee. The fee was more than the moped was worth so I called Detective Sasso.

"Jesus Christ," he began, "is *everybody* a crook?"

I remained silent.

"I'll take care of it," he assured me and hung up the phone.

An hour later I received a call from the Waltham Chief of Police. He apologized and said I could pick up the bike anytime. I picked it up that afternoon.

Donna suggested we should thank the detective, so she wrote a glowing letter to his District A supervisor, carefully worded to leave out certain uncomfortable details.

A week later I heard a commotion out in front of my house. I looked out the window to see Detective Sasso placing a revolving blue light on the top of his Crown Vic while stopped in the middle of the street.

"Go around the block God-damn it! Can't you see I'm parking here?" he yelled at the car behind him.

The doorbell rang and there was the detective, wearing his ill-fitting suit and holding out a bouquet of flowers.

"These are for your wife," he said.

He proceeded to tell us that in his twenty-one years as a cop he had never received such a letter and it was being put in his service record and he couldn't thank us enough.

"If you ever need anything, you be sure to call me," he said.

Sometimes I wish my life hadn't been so blessed, so that I might have had a reason to call him again.

Is Perfect Good Enough?

I've been a builder for forty-six years and two phrases often heard at a job-site are *good enough for government work* and *is perfect good enough? The former* reflects the sentiment of why do better than is expected and the latter voices the feeling that some clients are never satisfied.

Twenty-five years ago, I walked through a Beacon Hill townhouse that was slated to be renovated. The perspective client was walking beside me and was quite animated in describing what she desired. She was a successful businesswoman who my dad would have described as 'having more money than brains.'

"I've been trying to get this house for years and now I have it and I want it to be perfect," she said.

Perfect? I thought, *hmmm...*

"When you say *perfect*, what do you mean... *exactly*?" I asked.

"Well, the apartment where I'm living now is perfect," she answered without hesitating.

"Really..." I said, "could you show it to me?"

We walked a few blocks to her present apartment and I took a look around. It was a nice apartment, with reasonable workmanship but far from what I would call *perfect*.

"Could you show me something in here that isn't perfect," I requested.

"That wall," she offered and pointed without hesitation, "when the light hits it just right it doesn't look smooth and it drives me crazy."

I thought about trying to explain that shining a light (with its tiny wavelength) just right, would show anything to be not smooth; but didn't. I thought about telling her that nature is not perfect; that there is no such thing as flawlessness; that we can only approach perfection, but cannot attain it.

Instead I felt comfortable assuring her, "If this is perfect... then I do perfect."

But after hours (and days) discussing many details and contract issues with her, I began to have doubts; and wondered to myself, with this person *is perfect good enough*?

Clearly in the dictionary the definition of the word perfect leaves absolutely no leeway, but oddly enough, means different things to each of us.

I wisely didn't do that renovation but the discussion reminded me of my very first construction project. I was ten years old and my dad was having our new house built. He bought some land on Banks Street and decided on an off-the-shelf, architect-designed split level ranch. The lumber for the entire house was pre-cut and color coded at a factory in Ohio, then shipped on a huge flatbed truck. When it arrived, a telephone pole had to be removed so it could turn onto Banks Street. It was unloaded and stacked in the proper order at the site, then all that was necessary was for the contractor to refer to the plans. It was ready to build, so it would go together incredibly quickly. And it would have... if dad hadn't changed the length of the house by four feet and decided that it should all be on one level instead of split... *after it was delivered!* The two carpenters that Dad hired, Dominic and Joe, not only had to re-cut every pre-cut piece of lumber, but they had to figure out exactly which of the pieces to cut, and by how much.

It was a nightmare and took forever. The good news was that I got to spend a lot of time there helping out. Joe was the quiet one and definitely did most of the hard work while Dominic was outgoing, good natured, had a thick Italian accent and taught me a lot.

"You go get-eh me a stud. A straight-eh one. Okay?" he called out.

I had no idea how to tell if a two-by-four was straight or not. So I brought the top one over.

"What-sa this? I said a stud. Not a dogs hind leg."

He sighted along it's length and then tossed it aside.

"She's-eh no good. She's-eh gotta be perfetto," he told me.

"What?"

"You know. The best," he said.

"Why? No one will see it," I remarked sincerely.

"Why?... why? What's-eh matta you?" Dominic muttered then yelled to Joe, "He wants-eh know why she gotta be perfetto."

Joe, who was high up on a ladder, made an unfamiliar hand

gesture.

Dominic seemed pleased by his response and continued, "because it's-eh how you show the world who-eh you are. She's no perfetto, then you nobody."

After much trial and error, and many more rejected studs, I eventually figured out the technique.

They let me help with everything, which included using tools a ten year old should never have been allowed near. I spent a lot of time doing odd jobs, cleaning up, putting on band-aids and working inside of closets but after a while, I wanted to do more.

"Can't I do something that's not in a closet?" I asked Dominic.

"You wanna more work?" he said, "Let-eh me tell you something. You wanna know a good carpenter, you look-eh in the closets. Closets no good, carpenters no good."

"Not perfetto!" I said, waving my hands around like Joe would have.

"Si. Si. That's-eh right," he said with a big smile.

But after a minute I realized things weren't going to change, so I said, "Well, when can I do more stuff?"

He rubbed his chin.

"Okay then, you go up-eh the roof," he ordered.

I went up on the scaffolding and helped Joe with the roofing but made the mistake of bragging at supper that night. My mother had a conniption fit.

"Don't you ever do that again," she yelled, "If I find out—"

Dad interrupted and tried to calm her down.

"Wait a minute. You think everyone's like you?" Dad said, "How's he supposed to learn?"

"Learn what? How to fall off a roof and break a leg?" she asked in a somewhat calmer voice.

What I did learn was that as long as Mom didn't find out, I could pretty much do what I wanted to at that work site. I helped out every day during the summer. It was great fun, I learned a lot and I didn't break a leg.

Unfortunately, after I went back to school but before the house was finished, Joe fell off a ladder and hurt his back while Dominic cut off a finger with a circular saw. I can only imagine what my mother had to say to Dad about that.

The four foot shorter, single-level ranch was eventually finished and it turned out just fine (but not perfect.) I lived there until I went off to college.   . . .

I may be the only person on planet Earth who didn't watch the first Moon landing on TV. I was a high school teacher but during that summer I was living in and renovating a carriage house in the woods of Manchester-by-the-Sea, Massachusetts for my friend, Flip. The first couple of nights, Donna and I slept on rolls of insulation covered in a tarpaulin. She cooked on a wood burning stove (I guess we all weren't entering the Space Age in 1969.) It turned out well and in the fall I renovated my own Beacon Hill house, and that turned out well also.

So when I tired of teaching I decided to go into the construction business. I had done a couple of renovations, been house manager at the fraternity and worked with Dom and Joe on Banks Street; what else would I need?

A builder's license, for one thing. But catch-22 was in full force in Boston at the time. In order to apply for a license, you needed two years experience supervising construction; but you were not allowed to supervise construction without a license. So I 'stretched' my experience a bit on paper then passed the oral exam and I was on my way.

I had lots of work on Beacon Hill, got more skilled and competent at construction, but I could never quite get comfortable with the bureaucracy. As I began my career, many building inspectors in Boston were knowledgeable former contractors, but openly corrupt.

"Are you in charge here?" the inspector asked me gruffly.

"Yes sir," I answered.

He walked around looking at the new work then approached an untouched bathroom.

"What about this one?" he said, "Where's the permit for this one?"

"There is no permit. I didn't do anything in there," I replied, somewhat surprised by the question.

"That's what you say. I'm shutting this job down," he said with authority. He walked off and down the stairs.

I stood and looked around.

"What just happened?" I uttered aloud.

The plumber, who had been nearby, came up to me and said, "Go after him. Give him what he wants."

"What?" I said, stupidly.

"Jesus!... Wait here. I'll take care of it," he said as he turned and ran down the stairs.

Five minutes later he returned.

"All set. I gave him twenty bucks," he said as he walked away shaking his head, "Pay me back tomorrow."

"Twenty bucks? He risked his job for twenty bucks?" I said.

"They been doing it for years," the plumber yelled back to me. "It will never change."

But it did change. Over the next few years almost everyone I knew at the building department was indicted and more than a few went to jail. Suddenly the place was staffed with bureaucrats. They were honest but didn't know which end of a hammer to hold. I'm not sure which group was worse.

Some years later I had a wonderful job renovating and building an enormous house by a lake in Sherborn, Massachusetts. The client wanted a first class job and it took two and a half years.

He often asked, "Is there a better way to do this?"

And if there was, we did it.

One day at a job meeting I mentioned that a German-made lock specified by the architect had an equally good American made counterpart.

"and it's only $450 instead of $750," I said proudly.

The client, still wearing his coat and tie from the office, said, "What's your point?"

"Um... three hundred dollars," I replied, "...and I've seen it and it's just as good."

He studied me for a few seconds then said, "But *just as good* isn't perfect. I don't want to settle for *just as good*."

I thought, *What are you talking about?* but instead said, "No problem, we'll use the more expensive one."

He went away happy. That's when I was once again reminded that perfect, like everything else, is relative and sometimes only perfect is good enough.

My Weddings

When our friends, Cristina and Yates asked me to officiate at their wedding, I simply said, "I'm not a clergyman or a justice of the peace; how would I do that?"

"I'm pretty sure you can," Yates said, and to my amazement, I found out that Massachusetts (as well as a few other states) allows it. I filled out a form petitioning the Governor, got one letter of reference and I swore I was of high moral character. (When I asked what high moral character meant, I was told that it meant I wasn't convicted of a felony in the last two years.) A person who meets these conditions (and pays a $25 fee) is allowed to perform one wedding per year and gets the official title of wedding *solemnizer*.

Yates took me aside and had one more small request, "You figure out all the words... just promise me you won't mention God."

Sounded easy enough except that the bride's family would be traveling from Colombia to attend the ceremony and they were all devout Roman Catholics.

Hmm, I thought, *how to get God involved without mentioning his name.*

My relationship with God through the years has been at best, awkward. I was baptized, brought up as a Roman Catholic and removed from the public school the moment that Saint John the Evangelist parochial school was opened in our town. The Sisters of Saint Joseph had six years (from third grade to eighth) to convince me that I was a hopeless sinner and terribly in need of redemption. (The only redeeming I was aware of back then was for soda bottles at two cents each at Walsh's Drug store.) We were marched to confession each week and what with impure thoughts (I did sit behind Joan Carty after-all) and puberty lurking about, I found no end of things to confess to.

The dogma, like the *holy ghosts* and *virgin births,* was very confusing and I got seriously hung up on whether or not an all-powerful God could make a rock so heavy that he couldn't lift it. Just when science was helping me understand more and more, religion was telling me to stop asking so many questions.

So the wedding day arrived and I was sure Cristina's family was wondering who the hell was this bearded man (obviously not a priest) in the tuxedo and beard who was going to perform the ceremony? But a few days before the event; it had come to me. Yates was in Boston being treated for leukemia and Cristina was the reason he was going to make it. It was obvious to everyone what she was an *angel*. That was it. I would talk about... an angel!

Because of his illness, Yates couldn't be indoors with any large group of people so the ceremony took place outside in a park. The weather cooperated and there were quite a few people there including Yates's oncologist, Dr. Stone.

"Yates is so pleased you could attend," I said.

"I wouldn't miss it," he said, "usually I'm attending funerals. I prefer this."

"Well, I know Yates has to stay a safe distance from people and can't shake hands and such, but I was wondering if I could end the ceremony by letting him kiss the bride?"

Dr. Stone looked at me queerly and said, "Why? You think they haven't been kissing all this time?"

There were only two things that I was required by the State to say, to make it official; I had to ask them if they were doing this willingly and tell them under what authority they were being married. The rest was just fluff.

So after my little speech about what a great

Cristina, Yates, & Dr. Stone (2010)

couple they were, how happy I was that they let me marry them and Cristina, the angel; the couple recited their vows and affirmed they were doing this voluntarily with two *"I do's."*

Then I said, *"By the power vested in me by the Commonwealth of Massachusetts I hereby declare you to be husband and wife. And by the power vested in me by Dr. Stone, you may kiss the bride."*

Well, it's hard to describe what an amazing feeling it was... for me! They were really married! I said a few words and they were changed into married people. I felt like a magician who had just said *abracadabra* and pulled a rabbit out of a hat! It was so cool.

A friend suggested that if I liked it so much, I should do it for a living.

"I would, except I can only do one a year and I lose $25 each time," I replied.

Since then I've done three more weddings (two for my daughters) and it is still a high each time.

The only clear memory I have of my own wedding is how pretty Donna was in her short white sun dress, carrying daisies, coming down the aisle; and then the kiss at the alter. I wanted to be with her so badly that I'd have said and done whatever was necessary to get her. I don't even remember the vows (but I'm pretty sure I've kept them, whatever they were.)

Meeting Stephen Hawking

Imagine you walk into a supermarket, and in the fruit department you see Isaac Newton weighing a bag of apples. What would you do? Would you talk to him? What would you say?

"Thank goodness for gravity, eh Mr. Newton?"

In 1989, I was on Charles Street not far from my house. I needed a light bulb.

"Hi Dick," I said on entering the hardware store. The space around the register was unusually crowded. I could barely get to the counter and no one was moving.

"What's happening--"

Dick was not paying attention. He was craning his neck, looking toward the back of the store and he wasn't happy.

"What's up?" I asked again, while also looking in that direction.

"Some guy in a wheelchair blocking that aisle where the steps are. You'll have to wait a minute."

Norm, who was copying a key for a woman, didn't look up but said, "Scientist."

"What?" I said.

"Some scientist. I've seen him on TV," he replied, "Here you go ma'am. Be sure and try 'em when you get home."

He handed her some keys.

"Really?" I said aloud. *Scientist?* I thought.

Everyone was standing in front of the counter so I squeezed my way past a man holding a toilet plunger and into the next aisle over. Then walked to the back of the store past the cans of paint and up the two steps.

Scientist in a wheel chair? I thought as I turned up the obstructed aisle, *Dr. Strangelove perhaps.*

Up ahead was a wheelchair all right. It had a blue and yellow California license plate hanging on the back; *STEPHEN* it read. From the rear it appeared to be unoccupied until I got closer and could see a man slumped behind an odd computer keyboard contraption.

Standing next to the chair was a tall, twenty-ish blond man who looked at me and in a stage whisper said, "He can't go past a hardware store without going in."

The young man turned the wheelchair and its passenger slowly around to face me.

Oh my God, I thought.

There was no mistaking who it was.

"Stephen Hawking!" I said aloud before I could stop myself.

He didn't appear to react or to notice me so I wasn't sure what to do next, but his aide gestured reassuringly, so I began to speak.

"Eh... Hello... Professor Hawking. Sorry to bother you. I'm glad--"

There was no reaction at all from Hawking but the young man nodded for me to continue.

"I mean... It's an honor to meet you," I said, wishing I had said something more intelligent.

Nothing happened. The young man motioned for me to wait. Except for breathing, there appeared to be no movement in the wheelchair.

Then I heard his computer generated voice , *"Nice to meet you too."*

I looked at where the voice originated, then at the professor.

Hawking's eyes still appeared to be focused on the floor.

I wasn't sure where to look or what to say, so I thought back over all the physics courses I had taken at MIT and came up with, "Are you enjoying Boston?"

Looking more closely, I could now see that he was composing his answer using the tiniest motion of his thumb; it was barely perceptible.

While we waited, his aide added, "Professor Hawking is giving a lecture tonight at Northeastern University."

"I find Boston very interesting," the voice said, then after another pause, *"Perhaps you would like to come to my lecture tonight."*

I smiled and said, "Thank you. Thank you very much. I'll try. I hope it goes well."

I wasn't sure whether to wait for a response or not. His aide settled it by turning the wheelchair and pushing it toward the front of the hardware store and down the step.

The young man turned his head and said softly, "Just a heads up, I think it's sold out."

People gave way and someone held the door as Stephen Hawking and his aide went back out onto Charles Street. The store returned to normal.

I stood collecting my thoughts. In my sophomore year at college I went to a rock concert at Canobie Lake, New Hampshire and shook hands with Chuck Berry. I considered never washing my hand again. What is it about meeting famous people that captivates us? Who knows?

Now what did I come in here for? I wondered.

"Ah... light bulb!" I said aloud and went to get one.

"Do you know who that was?" I asked Dick when I got to the register. I didn't wait for an answer, "Stephen Hawking, that's who."

Dick leaned toward Norm and said, "Hey Norm, Is that who you thought? Stephen Hawkins?"

"Hawk-ing," I corrected, "He's been compared to Isaac Newton. Both physics professors at Oxford."

"Nice. That makes two geniuses who have never bought anything in here," he said.

I thought about going to the lecture at Northeastern that night, but I knew I probably wouldn't have gotten in and I was happy enough to have *actually met and talked with Stephen Hawking*!

Bongo

His given name was Robert but everyone called him Bongo. It had something to do with not being able to pronounce Robert correctly as a baby, but in fact, there is no way he was ever a Robert. He was Bongo.

He was a tile setter by trade and a fisherman by temperament. He often arrived a little late for jobs if the fishing was exceptionally good. He lived alone in the last surviving trailer park in the city of Boston and never tired of talking about it. He struggled with his weight but claimed to have a height problem.

"If I were just a few inches taller, I'd be the perfect weight," he lamented at coffee break.

Clients all liked him and craved his opinions and approval concerning tile and grout colors. He never had a bad word to say about anyone and I always looked forward to the days that he would be working at a job-site.

You could have been forgiven if you assumed he was gay, what with the colorful bandannas he wore and being single at fifty but I guess only his girlfriend, Annie, would know for sure.

He did have one secret that he kept for years. I found out about it one day when I asked him to once again help a client pick out a tile for her bathroom.

"Bongo, Linda needs help with the border tile upstairs. She thinks you're great, so would you give her some advice," I said.

He climbed the stairs and I heard them talking.

"A light green would go well with the field tile," he advised.

"Which of these is better?" she asked.

"Let me think on it for a minute," he said.

He came back down holding the two tiles and took me aside.

"Which of these is a light green?" he asked quietly.

"What?"

"Shhh! Not so loud. Which of these is a light green?" he repeated.

I stared at him.

"Okay, so I'm color blind," he said in a whisper, "No need to tell the world."

I pointed to a tile and he went back upstairs.

"This is the one you want," he told her.

"Oh, Bongo," she said, "You're always so good at picking just the right shade. You make it so easy."

And in fact, having a Bongo on a job, reassuring people, actually did make made things go a lot easier. Later, on that same job, the homeowner was having an argument with her husband about what color to paint the trim on the outside of the house. They called me over.

"Could you settle this for us?" the husband said, "Linda says green and I say white."

"You don't want to ask me," I said, "I'm the last person you should ask."

"No; we value your opinion," she said, "Green or white?"

"Well... I'd paint it white," I said without hesitation.

"That settles it then," said the husband, "Green it is!"

We painted it green and they loved it.

One day Bongo was struggling with a framing square while laying out floor tile.

"What are you doing?" I asked.

"I need to make this line 90 degrees from the center-line," he replied, "and I can't get it accurate enough."

"Use a magic triangle," I said, "You know, 3 – 4 – 5."

He looked up at me quizzically and shrugged. I proceeded to show him how it worked. He seemed very impressed.

"There's also the 5 – 12 – 13 triangle," I told him, "that works too."

"How do you know this stuff?" he asked.

"High school geometry; Pythagoras from ancient Greece figured it out," I said.

"Ah, that explains it," he said, "I'm Portuguese."

He took ill one day, went home early and was diagnosed with a blocked artery. After an operation he returned to work in a few weeks, but was put on a special diet.

"They told me I could only have twelve hot dogs a year," he lamented. Then got a little sparkle in his eye and said, "I'm having 4 of them tonight."

He made wine in his brother's basement, asked everyone for empty wine bottles, used duct tape to make labels and gave everyone at the job a bottle of red wine.

"I call it *Chateau du Duct Tape,*" he said.

We were not thrilled at the thought of homemade wine, but out of guilt Donna and I tried it that night and incredibly, it was terrific.

It was so good that I actually thought, *If he can make wine this good at home, maybe I should try.*

The following year, Chateau du Duct Tape arrived and it was indescribably dreadful; thus ended any thoughts of wine making in my basement.

More than once, Bongo mentioned that his father had passed away at 54 years old and a brother at 53, both from heart attacks. Then at 55, almost like genetic clockwork, Bongo got sick. Not the heart attack he feared, but cancer. He got weaker, stopped working and was soon in the hospital. I visited a few times and we tried to keep the conversation light, making up a scheme to sneak hamburgers up the fire escape into the hospital room or retelling the color-blind story, but he kept getting weaker and there was no cure. He decided that he wanted to return to his home. Two days before he died, I called and asked if I could visit him in his beloved trailer.

"Sure," he said, "bring some milk and a six pack of beer. And just come in, 'cause I can't get up."

There are no street signs in a trailer park and they all pretty much look alike so it took a while to find his. I hoped I was walking into the right one.

"Bongo, I brought the stuff you asked for," I yelled as I opened the door..

He looked up from his bed at the far end of the trailer and said weakly, "Thanks, put the milk in the frig."

"What about the beer?" I asked.

"Oh, that's for you," he said with a grin, then with some effort, held up a small pill bottle, "I have Oxycontin."

We talked a bit. Remarkably he made an effort to be upbeat and we made plans for my next visit in a few days.

When I entered the funeral home for the wake and saw that Annie had set up his fishing gear next to the casket, I started to bawl. She came over and hugged me.

"I'm supposed to console *you*," I sobbed, "I feel like an idiot."

"You know, he used to tell me that you were the smartest person he knew," she confided, "He called you *the professor* and he never got over that triangle thing you taught him."

We both stood there and cried for a while. I still keep his number in my contacts' list on my phone.

He's a hard guy to let go of.

In Memory of

Robert A. "Bongo" Agostinho

January 21, 1952
August 18, 2008

God saw you getting tired,
and a cure was not to be,
so He put His arms around you
and whispered "Come to Me."
With tearful eyes we watched
you,
and saw you pass away,
and although we loved you dearly,
we could not make you stay.
A golden heart stopped beating,
hard working hands at rest.
God broke our hearts to prove to
us,
He only takes the best.

Earthquake

The old saying, '*you can't fall off the floor*', implies that there's always something you can rely on, something you can trust beneath you. But what if you can't. We had a fire in our house when I was a little kid and we all ran outside and stood on the ground because obviously we would be safe *there*. But what if we weren't? What if you can't even count on the rock solid ground?

The Earth's crust, that we stand on, is only a few meager miles thick, below which is 4000 miles of swirling, molten rock, reaching a temperature of 5000 degrees centigrade. It's pure self-delusion that permits us to go about our daily routine on the surface. Nature cruelly allows us decades to get comfortable then at 4:31 in the morning... Ka-Boom! The ground suddenly slips and moves ten feet north and is lifted up a few feet. Pent up energy is released (the equivalent of many hydrogen bombs) and that energy starts moving at the speed of sound in rock (which is pretty fast!). The mass distribution of the planet alters slightly, changing the rotational speed of the Earth. The day is now 1.6 microseconds longer, the mountains outside of LA are 30 inches higher and 100,000 people are afraid to go back into their houses. Elevated highways have collapsed, gas lines ruptured and electric towers fallen. What was the 3rd floor of an apartment building is suddenly the 2nd floor; the former 2nd floor is now a tomb. Darkened light poles sway, swimming pools empty while people stand shifting their weight from leg to leg to stay upright on their front lawns as the motion slowly dampens. Even when the ground is no longer moving, people aren't so steady. Water could still be heard sloshing in the pools and light poles still appeared to be swaying. We were later told that the ground only shook for thirty-five seconds. Which means that by the time we woke up in the dark, figured out that we'd been thrown out of our bed and onto the floor, cleared our heads enough to remember we were visiting our son, his wife and one week old grandson in LA, found our shoes so we wouldn't get cut on the broken glass and made our way in the dark, down the stairs (which we weren't even sure were still there) and got outside... the earthquake was over.

But the ordeal had really just begun. The seven of us (and one newborn) made it outside and sat stunned, crammed into our rental car trying to figure out what was next. Zac had a broken his front tooth from a falling bureau and there was some anxiety because Jesse hadn't cried, but it turned out that he had just slept through it all! Jennifer was shaken up and, being a new mother, it would take her weeks to get over the shock. Kouri and her boyfriend stayed huddled together and Chloe was thankful that the large heavy TV that fell from its cabinet, had barely missed her head as she slept on a mattress on the floor.

We were all okay, but then we noticed fires breaking out all around us.

"Just broken gas lines," someone said in a failed attempt to comfort us.

For a moment I feared the worst. I checked to see how much gasoline was in the car and wondered if we could make it across the dessert if we had to.

With the power out throughout the city, the car radio could only pick up a station in San Francisco informing Angelinos that they had just endured a 6.8 earthquake. Then everything began moving again. Not as violently as before but everyone still got very anxious and quiet except for one woman, standing out on her lawn, who screamed.

"It's okay. It's just an aftershock," someone yelled, trying to keep everyone calm.

It was the first of maybe fifty that were felt in the next days.

Abruptly a helicopter appeared above with a searchlight sweeping the front lawns crowded with people clutching blankets and each other.

"Does anyone need assistance?" a bullhorn asked.

How impressive, I thought, *emergency teams are already out.* Then it hit me. *Why am I sitting here?*

Zac and I got a few of his hand tools and went around to see if we could help. We turned off some water and gas lines, but amazingly the fires were being brought under control and we saw no physically injured people. But psyches were another matter.

Aftershocks got so commonplace that soon we would

unconsciously stop and brace ourselves against a wall or a fence and wait for the motion to pass and then guess its Richter number. *(The scale is logarithmic so a 6.8 earthquake is 630 times more powerful than a 5.0 and the most powerful ever recorded was a 9.5).*

"I'll bet that was a 5.0," I called out then waited for the radio announcer to say, "We have a report of another aftershock... 4.9 this time."

"Hey, I'm getting pretty good at this," I said with some pride.

People remained jittery and many would not return inside their homes. An aftershock out on the lawn was one thing; but inside, with plates rattling, books falling and chandeliers swinging was another. And the elephant in the room was that no one knew if another *big one* would occur.

We spent the day righting the furniture, putting things back on shelves, cleaning the house and looking for the cat. (The cat remained missing for a couple of days until it crawled out of the bed's box-spring foundation.)

As evening arrived, we had gas and water but the phone lines were out and still no electricity. Candles were lit and Donna began to boil water for pasta. Fortunately she had done a huge food shopping run the day before to fill the larder for the kids and as darkness fell, a combination of cooling temperature and a desire to not be alone caused people from around the neighborhood to began to drift in. Soon we had twenty or more virtual strangers in the house and after eating, they showed no sign of wanting to leave. So we dragged mattresses out on the floor in the living room and the hall (some people actually brought their own) and got as comfortable as we could. I attempted to sleep sitting up against a wall in the hall with the help of a sofa cushion but I mostly watched the assembled refugees. One woman had a newborn even younger than two week old Jesse. What a welcome into the world.

About four A.M. I heard a noise coming from the kitchen. I got up to see what it was and noticed out of the window that the traffic lights had all just come on. Green lights as far as the eye could see down the main street; then they all turned yellow... then red together. What a sight. The noise turned out to be the refrigerator motor. We all had electricity again. Over the course of the morning, Donna made breakfast (oatmeal I think) for the horde and then they slowly drifted away. We heard reports that the major highways nearby had collapsed and travel would be difficult. If it hadn't been the Martin Luther King Jr. Holiday, the death toll from the fallen roadways would have been much higher.

   Pretty soon we hardly paid attention to the aftershocks. Some reports said there had been hundreds! People are amazingly resilient (or maybe stupid...) and soon things appeared to get back to normal. Donna and I stayed on for a week or so then eventually drove the alternate route back to the airport.

   New England hasn't had a destructive earthquake since 1755 so we think the Earth is pretty reliable here. It probably isn't, but what matters is that Zac and Jennifer *think* it is and so they moved back east with my grandson soon after.

Car Salesmen

Is there anything more baffling in this life than figuring out how to buy a new car? From my Triumph TR4 roadster on, each attempted purchase has been a completely unique experience with different rules and fraught with unexpected twists and turns. But there was one constant; the car salesman.

When we moved to Beacon Hill with its limited parking and our limited budget, I reluctantly sold my TR4 to my friend, Bill Morton. I had a Yamaha motorcycle for a while then when a client whose house I was renovating in the South End couldn't pay me, he gave me his beat-up 1960 faded green Ford F-150 pickup truck. It had a hole so big in the floor boards that small children weren't allowed near it and you had to be careful where you put your feet but it managed to survive for a year or so. When it died, I decided I wanted a new pickup truck so Donna's dad, Eddie, who was an Oldsmobile salesman, called a friend of his at a Dodge dealership.

"He'll take care of you," he said, "but don't let him sell you undercoating. It's a rip-off."

He was full of automotive *pearls of wisdom* like that.

All I wanted (or could afford) was a simple stripped down vehicle, so the process in the Dodge showroom went along quickly until near the end. We were filling out the paperwork when the salesman looked up.

"Oh, by the way... do you want a rear bumper," he asked.

I thought for a moment then said, "Isn't it the law that a truck has to have a rear bumper?"

"Oh, in Massachusetts yes," he answered.

"Well, aren't we in Massachusetts?"

"So I take it you want one then?"

"Well, yes," I said still a little bewildered.

"It's a ninety dollar extra," he informed me.

"Does it have a steering wheel?" I asked (only half joking.)

"Of course."

"Well that's good," I said sarcastically.

He continued unfazed (as car salesmen are unaffected by

sarcasm).

"We should find a truck for you in a day or two," he said, "Just tell me what color you want."

"Oh, I don't care what color as long as it has the couple of options I told you."

"Well, what colors do you *prefer*?"

"Really, I don't care what color it is," I repeated.

"Okay, I'll call when we find one," he said.

Two days later the phone rang.

"Well, we found your truck," the salesman said.

"What color is it?" I asked.

"Santa Fe Tan," he replied enthusiastically.

"Oh-no," I cried, "That's the only color I can't stand."

The phone was silent for a moment, then the voice said, "But you told me--"

Ah, a little taste of your own medicine, I thought. "Don't worry," I said, "I did tell you I didn't care... I'll live with it."

It was truly an awful color but I did live with it until my daughter Chloe arrived and the only way the whole family could ride together was with someone in the truck bed. So we bought a 1984 Dodge van and I could travel with my whole family *and* my tools.

Since then, not only have the prices skyrocketed (the van was the last vehicle we owned that cost me less than $10,000) but the whole process changed again. I used to tell the salesman what I wanted, now the salesman tells me what I can have.

A few years ago I was purchasing a Toyota RAV4 and the only option I wanted was leather seats... that's all... just leather seats.

"That's easy enough," said the salesman, "and that comes with a moon-roof, six CD changer and 10 speaker audio system, power mirrors and keyless ignition. An eighteen hundred dollar extra."

"But I don't want a moon-roof," I said.

"If you want leather seats, you do."

So I ended up with a moon-roof (or is it a sun-roof?)

My most memorable encounter with a car salesman was in 1994. Donna and I decided we needed a vehicle that was more like a car than the van I had been driving for ten years so we ended up at York Motors looking at Isuzu Troopers.

"You've come to the right place," the salesman said, "What do we have to do to get you into a new Trooper?"

"Not much," I replied, "I'll tell you what I want; if you have it and we agree on a price, I'll buy it."

It seemed simple enough to me.

The salesman looked like he had just come from central casting; mid fifties, slicked back hair, thin mustache, loud sport coat.

"I can give you an incredible deal on a brand new white Trooper," he offered.

"I definitely don't want a white one," I said, "I don't plan to sell ice cream."

I proceeded to give him my modest list of needs.

"Let me check my stock," he said and off he went to places unknown.

A few minutes later he was back and began, "We don't have exactly what you want but I can offer you a terrific deal on a really sweet white Trooper with--"

"I do not want a white Trooper... or a white anything for that matter," I interrupted, "I told you what I want. If you don't have one I'll just--"

He was undaunted and continued, "You've come to the right place. I definitely can get you what you want. Let me just check on something."

And off he went again.

"There must be two hundred cars out there on the lot. Why don't they ever have the car I want?" I asked rhetorically.

Donna wisely didn't respond.

He reappeared and began as if we had never spoken before, "We are prepared to paint the white Trooper any color you want... for cost."

Donna and I just stared at him.

"Okay, I get it. Give me one more chance," he pleaded and was gone in an instant.

"This is stupid," I said to Donna, "Let's get out of here."

Donna looked lost in thought.

"He looks so familiar," she said, "doesn't he?"

I shrugged my shoulders and answered, "Not really."

"I've seen him somewhere," she said "I know I have."

He returned with some papers and started right in, "Here's what we can do," and slid a sheet over for me to see.

It listed a Trooper with the options I wanted and a price of $24,500.

"That's more than I want to pay," I said and began to stand up.

"We're losing money at that price," he said, "It has to be shipped here and-- "

"Well thanks for your time but if that's the best you can--"

"Did you ever drive a limousine?" Donna exclaimed out of the blue.

"What?" the salesman said.

"Drive a limousine; say thirty years ago?" she asked.

"I did for a while, yes. In the sixties. Why?"

"You drove us from the church in Winthrop to our reception at Polcari's Italian restaurant in the North End in nineteen... sixty..."

"Sixty-six," I reminded her.

"Oh my god! You're not Eddie's daughter?" he boomed.

"It's me," she said.

"Look at you! You haven't changed a bit," he gushed, "And how is Eddie? I haven't seen him in years."

He reminisced about the good old days, selling used cars with Eddie and driving a limo then a serious expression appeared on his face.

"Give me that," he said as he pulled the sheet from my hand, "I'll be right back."

And once more he disappeared.

A moment later he placed a paper on the table and said, "How does that look?"

"Twenty thousand?" I read aloud, "Looks... fine, thanks"

We signed some papers, talked a little more about the wedding then he told me I could pick up the car in a few days.

"See; he wasn't such a bad guy," Donna said as we drove home in the van.

"Hmm, maybe," I replied.

The following week I arrived at the dealership and didn't notice a white Trooper anywhere on the lot so before I drove off in my new green one, I made damn sure it had original factory paint.

The Count Lipsky Affair

The Chelsea Hotel was the most "in" hotel in the most "in" city in the world. If you knew just a little about the people who have stayed at this New York City landmark you could teach twentieth century history at any university. To name just a few of the famous clientele: Jack Kerouac wrote "On the Road" there, Mark Twain boarded there, Bob Dylan, Sid Vicious and The Grateful Dead composed music there, Arthur C. Clarke wrote "2001" there, Janis Joplin and John-Paul Sartre slept there (but not together) and on and on. Thus it should come as no surprise that Donna and I wanted to stay there.

We lived in Boston and liked it well enough, but New York City was, well... the epitome of cool. So in the spring of 1971, we drove the 250 miles to lower Manhattan with Bill Morton and his wife and took up residence for the weekend at the iconic hotel. It was built in 1885 and looked every day of it. It was run-down, frayed and dirty as well as home to various unregistered vermin.

But New York had such an allure, and Donna and I being young, we overlooked the fact that the city (and the hotel for that matter) was bankrupt, crime ridden and just about out of control. It was of such huge scale that it was hard to not be in awe. Where Boston had one store that sold pens, New York City had *three blocks* of such stores! The city had seven million people; more than the *states* of Massachusetts, New Hampshire, Vermont and Maine combined and incredibly more than thirty-five of the other fifty states. New York City's police department was larger than the army of Belgium. The Yankees always seemed to win while the Red Sox never did. It had the tallest building in the world and the second tallest building in the world. It was the stuff of legend.

So here we were in the *Big Apple* where we attended a jazz club, had lunch in a real Jewish deli and walked to the Brooklyn Bridge. Then we visited Barry, a Boston friend who had taken a job at the architectural office of I.M. Pei where he was helping design the sixty-story John Hancock tower to be built in Boston. We met him at a cafe in Greenwich Village after which he proudly showed us his apartment. It was up a number of steps on the first floor of a brownstone and very tiny. Kitchen counter space was provided by a piece of plywood placed over the sink. The only way into the bedroom was through the bathtub. The door to the apartment was solid steel with a variety of locking mechanisms none of which prevented an incident that had occurred the previous month.

Arriving home from work one evening he found a man standing in the hall outside of his flat. When Barry had completely unlocked the door, the man pushed him into the apartment, duct taped him to a kitchen chair, gagged him and proceeded to try on all his clothes as he watched helplessly. After berating Barry's taste in apparel and shoes, the man left carrying an armful of items. Still attached to the chair, Barry bounced over to the open apartment door, out into the hall and finally to the front door of the building. With great effort, he managed to get the front door open by partly standing with his back to the door, raising his bound hands to the height of the doorknob, and leaning against the heavy oak slab. It slowly swung out and unable to stop himself, Barry and the piece of furniture together tumbled down the ten steps of the stoop to the pavement, coming to rest on his right side, facing the street. Someone who had likely seen his fall, walked alongside.

"Pleeth Helth Meeh," Barry tried to call out despite the gag.

The man continued by without slowing; as did the next three people.

Finally a woman stopped, bent down and asked, "Do you need some help, young man?"

"Yeth!" Barry said.

We were astounded that so many people had ignored his plight, but Barry said he was actually lucky and that if he had lived uptown it would have taken at least ten people before someone helped.

"But the worst thing was," Barry lamented, "that the robber weighed thirty pounds more than me. None of my clothes could possibly fit him!"

Later that evening he suggested we go out to eat at his favorite restaurant.

"It's a little pricey," he said, "but you don't come to New York to save money."

We hopped in two cabs and soon were seated at a center table ordering drinks. It was one of those restaurants where the waiters were much better dressed than the patrons. We talked a bit while sipping our wine and reading the menu (and noted that he wasn't kidding about it being pricey.)

Suddenly a voice called out, "Oh, by all that's holy! Can that be you?"

It was a tall man, in his fifties sporting a Van Dyke beard and wearing a long black cape.

"Surely you remember me," he almost pleaded, "Lipsky... Count Lipsky."

He took a grand bow, swishing his cape as he did.

We all looked at each other.

Then without hesitation he said, "Allow me to introduce my lady; Madam Florence."

Tall, much younger, blonde and attractive, Florence nodded as Count Lipsky pulled a seat away from an empty table and arranged it for her to sit next to Barry. Then he slid another chair over for himself as Bill Morton made room for him.

The waiter came over with two more place settings, brought more wine and took our orders.

Barry, who appeared a little nervous since his friend arrived said, "We're splitting the bill tonight--"

"Of course, of course. What a marvelous idea," said the Count, "I'd have it no other way."

We talked about the new plays in town, how much we disliked Richard Nixon and what it must be like to work for I. M. Pei.

"I haven't met him yet," Barry admitted, "It's a big office."

Then we talked at length about the pros and cons of rent control.

The Count and his lady friend nodded a lot but didn't add much to the conversation.

Not wanting to embarrass Barry, no one asked how Lipsky came to be royalty but we enjoyed looking at Florence in her low cut dress and we all had a nice meal. More wine, dessert and finally coffee followed, then the check was placed on the table.

Barry did some calculations then told us that since this was his favorite restaurant and he wanted to stay in their good graces he was adding in a decent tip.

"So, it comes to thirty-two dollars per person," he announced.

Credit cards were not common then, so most restaurant bills were paid in cash. Barry took out his thirty-two dollars and handed it to me. I added three twenties and a five then removed a one and handed the pile to Bill who added his and handed it on to the Count; then back to Barry who dutifully straightened out the wad and tallied it.

"Hey, it's sixty dollars short!" he reported.

A bit stunned, we all looked around the table at each other. I figured it had to be the Count but I wasn't going to be the one to accuse Barry's friend of cheating us. The silence was painful.

Then Bill broke the ice and said, "Look, let's just each put in ten dollars more and call it a night."

And that's what we did, being careful to watch as Count Lipsky put his two tens on the table. No one had much to say to the Count as he swished his cape, bowed and walked off with Madam Florence. Then the five of us quietly made our way out of the restaurant.

Out front, Bill Morton asked Barry, "Where in hell did you ever meet that guy?"

Barry stopped trying to hail a cab, turned and replied, "Meet him? I don't know him. I thought he was a friend of yours!"

Everyone remained quiet for a few minutes then we said goodnight to Barry, wished him well, cabbed back to the Chelsea Hotel, checked for bedbugs and went to sleep.

33 years later, the Boston Red Sox finally beat the Yankees.

Real Estate

"The whole building is scheduled for demolition next spring," the realtor said without looking up from her desk, "but you could have a month-to-month lease if you like,"

We stepped back and Donna whispered to me, "It's perfect and so cheap."

"That's because it's going to be torn down in a few months," I said.

"But we need a place fast," Donna was quick to remind me.

"And you don't exactly have great references," the realtor, who had obviously overheard us interjected, *"Starting a job next Monday* and *undergraduate student* doesn't look that spectacular on a rental application."

"We'll take it," we said in unison.

We had returned from our honeymoon just four days before and this was the third apartment we had looked at. We moved in to the second floor front, two bedroom apartment in September of 1966 and paid $125 per month rent. (And despite the warning about its imminent destruction, that apartment house on Commonwealth Avenue at Berkeley Street is still standing!) It was a five story building with high ceilings, working fireplaces and an open cage elevator that we hardly ever used (except to visit Toddy and Flip on the third floor). It was where Wild Bill roamed the hallways at all hours, creeping everyone out.

The larger twelve foot high room with a great view of the Commonwealth Avenue mall was our bedroom, living room and dining room. It was furnished with a table and chairs at the windows and had a big rectangular bed / couch that I made, sitting in the middle. We had a tiny kitchen with no windows (it had a refrigerator that burned natural gas and sent soot all over) and a tiny bathroom with no windows. And in the smaller room, that some might call a closet with a window, lived Zoe, our 16 year-old foster daughter. We had Snoopy, a wire haired fox terrier that had been my present to Donna on our first Christmas, and Oscar Wilde, a white cat that Zoe and Donna adopted from the Animal Rescue

League. Donna worked at MIT as an office manager/secretary, I was teaching high school nearby and Zoe was a high school student. I still had a Triumph TR4 roadster and a motorcycle. Life was very good.

So one day, Flip, who was now working at a big downtown law firm said, "One of the partners at the firm is selling an apartment house on Beacon Hill. Why don't we look at it and see if we can't fix it up. We could each live in half."

That was February, 1969 when we went and looked. It was small, dirty, cockroach infested and located three doors from an infamous heroin dealer... but otherwise fine. Flip immediately lost interest.

I went home and described it to Donna in all of its depressing detail, and without hesitation she said, "Well... couldn't you fix it up?"

"I guess I could," I said with some uncertainty.

The next thing I knew I was talking to my father, getting advice about buying my first house.

"How much is he asking," dad inquired.

"$42,000," I said.

"Offer him thirty-six," he said.

"But he said--"

"Never mind what he said. You offer thirty-six. Then he'll say forty. Then you counter with thirty-eight and he'll say, 'okay let's make it thirty-nine.' See! You just saved three thousand dollars."

I must admit it all made sense when he said it, but the next day in the law firm's conference room, things didn't quite go that way.

"I'm prepared to offer $36,000," I said.

"Is there something wrong with your hearing?" he said, "I said the price is $42,000.

"$38,000?" I said.

He just stared at me, so I proceeded to tell him about the advice my dad had given me.

He pondered for a moment then said, "Okay. $41,500. That's as low as I go, and I'm only doing it for your father."

Donna and I emptied the top two floors when the leases came up and I worked there evenings, weekends and all summer. I had help from Bill Morton, my fraternity brother who now lived nearby. He had a way of making monotonous tasks seem like an adventure and the addition of his muscle and brain helped make it possible. Donna and I ended up with a two-bedroom apartment above three rental units. We shoveled up the hypodermic needles in the backyard, pestered the police to harass the drug dealers so they would move on, and over time, managed to get the teens to stop playing midnight basketball in the park next door.

Zac was born, Zoe went to off to college and then Kouri arrived. Life was very good.

One minor problem was that the apartment building next door was occupied by young people who were all aspiring to either be alcoholics or in a rock band. And if that wasn't bad enough, the woman in the basement studio apartment kept six or eight Russian wolf hounds. And if that still wasn't bad enough, she hadn't paid her rent for months, so the landlord cut off her electricity and water! It wasn't pretty.

There was always a party going on or a drum solo or a pack of dogs howling and more than once I was heard to say, "We should buy that building and get rid of those god-damned people."

Then one Sunday, Donna was reading The Globe real estate section and said, "There's a building for sale that sounds just like the building next door. Maybe we should call the number and find out."

The next morning we did and she was right. I went to the seller's office and he was obviously tired of owning an apartment house with all its problems, so right there, he agreed to sell it to me for $43,000. I called Flip and he dictated an *agreement to purchase* document over the phone that we signed. The next day the phone rang. It was the seller.

"I'll give you $10,000 to tear up our agreement," he said.

That was a lot of money in 1972, so I called Flip and asked why I shouldn't take it.

"Why would he offer you that kind of money unless it's worth a lot more than you're paying," he said, "He signed the agreement and has to sell it to you... or we'll sue his ass."

At the closing, the seller admitted, that the afternoon after he agreed to sell the building to me, he got an offer of $75,000!

As the leases came up we got five new tenants and much needed peace and quiet.

Three years later we emptied the top three floors and I renovated them, leaving two rental units below.

We moved into the new building and I eventually sold the first building for two and a half times what I paid for it and considered myself a genius. (It's now easily worth more than fifteen times even that!)

Now we had four bedrooms and a roof deck. Along came our third child, Chloe.

We soon incorporated the first floor into our unit. Now we had four floors.

Life was very good.

One by one the kids grew up and moved away, then Donna said, "Wouldn't it be nice to have a little house by a lake... ?"

So we spent many a weekend driving around New Hampshire, looking at shacks, making offers on *fixer uppers* and getting nowhere. Then while accompanying Zac (as chairman of the Westford Board of Health) on a visit to a new project in his town, we found a perfect little house by a lake, the aptly named *Long Sought For Pond*.

I mentioned my interest to the saleswoman and she informed me that the cottage I wanted, had been sold.

"But just in case, leave your phone number," she said.

A week later I got a call at work.

"That cottage is on the market again," she said, "If you want it just get us a deposit."

I was pretty busy at work so I called Zac and asked if he could go over and write out a check to hold the place until I could get there in a few days.

"Sure I can give them a check," he said, then paused. "Does it have to be good?"

"No I don't think so," I told him, "they'll just hold it until I get there."

That was eleven years ago and life is still very good.

Two Waiters

This is a story of two waiters who overcame adversity and succeeded against great odds. In one instance the foe was the Soviet Union and in the other it was the Central Grille All-Stars.

In 2012, Donna and I, and two friends were sitting at a table in a restaurant and after some considerable discussion we had reached four different conclusions.

"Definitely Russian," was one.

"No way. He's German I think," was another.

"Greek maybe."

And finally, "I'll bet he's Sardinian."

"Well there's only one way to find out," I said, "I'll ask him."

The waiter who had seated us was wearing a tuxedo, appeared to be in his seventies and spoke with an accent that none of us could place. I caught his eye and called him over.

"We were wondering where you are from. We don't recognize you accent," I said.

"Ah," he replied, "May I sit down?" He pulled out the end chair and got comfortable. "Let me tell you a story," he began.

We all leaned forward.

"When I was a very young man, my country was invaded by the Soviets-- "

"Czechoslovakian! I knew it," my friend called out.

"No, I said I was a very young man at the time, not middle aged. Now hear me out. My country was overrun with Russian tanks and my older brother Taavi and I had had enough, so we decided to escape. We took all the money we had and went to get false papers and airplane tickets."

He looked at each of us in turn and it was obvious he enjoyed retelling his adventure.

He continued, "It was very dangerous and the Soviet soldiers would have killed us if we were caught. We found the local militia and they asked us, '*Where do you want to go?*' We held out the money and said, '*As far as this will take us in America!*' So two days later we landed in Detroit. We spoke very little English but had a little book to translate phrases. We walked down the stairs from the plane and looked across at the terminal; there was America; all bright lights and neon signs... and no tanks.

Taavi asked me, *What does that neon sign say?* so I looked in my book.

Oh no, we have made a terrible mistake! I said to him, *I'm afraid we have come to the wrong country, Taavi. It says Hot Dogs.*

Then we both said in unison, *They... eat... dogs... here?!*"

The table erupted in laughter. The waiter stood up, pushed his chair toward the table and finished, "Now I am an American but that was 1956 and I came from..."

"Hungary," Donna said.

"Very good... and bon appetit." he said, "I will send over the waiter for this table."

I don't remember what we ordered that night but hot dogs would have probably been more appropriate.

. . .

Years earlier another waiter in a tuxedo was standing at my table. Seven compatriots and I, who attend the Boston Red Sox Fenway Park opening day game every year (and have for the past fifty years) were about to have dinner after playing a scrimmage baseball game at ten o'clock in the morning, then having *refreshments* at my Uncle Johnnie's bar (The Central Bar and Grille) in East Boston, where we proudly sported our Central Grille All-Star shirts. (Most of our time there was spent discussing the effect that eating Uncle Johnie's sausages would have on our digestive system the next day.) This was followed by the Red Sox game and finally ending up with a limousine ride to a private dining room in Locke Ober's Restaurant where the tuxedo clad waiter in question took our order.

Paul requested a pitcher of beer.

"I'm sorry. We don't serve pitchers of beer," the waiter informed.

Paul who was already quite inebriated, was taken aback.

"Do you serve pitchers of *water*," he asked.

"Yes, of course."

"Do you serve beer," Paul asked.

"Yes, in bottles."

"Then bring us a pitcher of water, but first... pour out the water and pour in ten bottles of beer."

"I'm afraid I can't do that," the waiter replied.

"Okay. Then please bring me ten open bottles of beer."

The waiter left, Paul looked around the room and spied a glass vase of plastic flowers on the window sill. Reaching over, he dumped the flowers onto the floor, blew vigorously into the glass container to clear out a month or two worth of dust and waited patiently.

The waiter returned with the tray of beer bottles and Paul commenced pouring their contents into the vase. The waiter, clearly defeated, regained his composure and proceeded to take our food order. As the evening went on, the waiter did his best to comply with our various (and sometimes senseless) demands.

One of the opening day regulars was unable to attend (which is seriously frowned upon) so to make amended he sent, in his stead, a stripper/belly dancer. Half way through the meal, in walks a young woman, carrying a boombox and she proceeds to disrobe, turn on some music and dance around the room. More than one waiter opened the door and peeked in to see what all the hootin' an' hollerin' was about. The performance ended and as she was dressing we found out she was a schoolteacher in a local town which triggered more than one schoolboy / fourth grade teacher fantasy. A few minutes later, she left without incident and our waiter reappeared. After clearing the entrees (and surely realizing he was almost rid of us) he took our dessert order and left; at which point, Flip decided to tell an elaborate story (perhaps motivated by the stripper?) which involved much animation. He moved around the room acting out the narrative which was about to culminate with him throwing open the door to the hallway and yelling, "Please come back, I have two pickets to Titsbourg!" But as fate would have it, at that instant the waiter had just returned holding a full tray of desserts. As Flip threw the door open, there was a loud cacophony of various sounds; metal tray, glass dishes, silverware, cups and saucers, and perhaps an "Ooh."

Then silence, as Flip slowly and softly pulled the door shut and tip-toed back to his seat. We all sat hands folded in front of us as we listened to the clean-up activities just outside. The minutes passed quietly then there was a sound at the door.

<Knock, knock>

"Come in," someone said in a very submissive tone.

<Knock, knock>

"Come in," was repeated.

The door opened an inch or two and an eye peered in. Then the door cautiously swung aside and in walked our waiter, still attired in his tuxedo but now colorfully adorned with strawberry parfait and whipped cream, hot fudge and coffee stains.

Mustering every ounce of his inner strength he served us our desserts and when finished, asked, "Will that be all... *gentlemen?*"

We all cringed when he uttered that last word. He departed the room with his head held high.

We finished and as we walked down the hall toward the lobby, we were met by the maitre d' (in his still pristine tuxedo) who said, "We would be very pleased if we never see you here again. And be assured, we will remember who you are."

Jim, Paul, Becker, Flip, Nathaniel, me, Zac, Jaramie, Jesse
50th year of Central Grill All-Stars (2017)

There you have it. Two waiters, two difficult, trying situations and two triumphs. And as for the Central Grille All-Stars; where some would have taken being asked to never return to Locke Obers as a blow to their dignity and honor, I believe we showed our true intellectual level and mental age that night-- we wore it as a badge of honor.

Checkmate

I was about to turn sixty-five years old, I was in good health and working every day. Things were going well. Then I received a letter from the Social Security Administration advising me that I was required to sign up for Medicare. There's a SSA office a few blocks from my house and I like to walk, so I headed over there one bright spring afternoon. I entered the O'Neill Federal office building, passed through the metal detector and walked up the one flight to the Social Security office where I was met by a rather corpulent uniformed security guard standing in the doorway.

"Can I help you," he asked.

"No thank you," I said, "I'm just here to sign up for Medicare."

"Do you have an appointment?"

"Appointment? No, I got a letter telling me I had to sign up; so here I am."

"Not without an appointment."

I looked past him and observed a sea of desks full of people, all apparently signing up for Medicare.

"Where can I make an appointment," I asked.

"By phone," he replied sternly.

"Well, I'm here now. Could I make an--"

"By phone," he repeated even more sternly.

"Do you happen to know the number," I inquired, "I'll call from my cellphone."

"You can find the phone number on the website," he said, obviously failing to grasp the growing humor of the situation.

I looked wistfully through the glass partition at my fellow citizens happily joining the Medicare ranks before I walked down to the lobby, where I sat and took out my phone. After playing *'can you guess which menu number to push'* a few times, I was instructed to hold for the next available agent. *<music> <music> <Your call is important to us, please hold... > <music><music>,* then finally ...

"This is Mrs. Fribish, in the Albequerque office speaking, how may I help you?"

I explained that I would like an appointment (but not in New Mexico) and she told me I could register right over the phone. So we began. Name, address and so on.

At city of birth, she stopped and apologized.

"I'm needed in another office," she said, "I'll have to transfer you to another agent and I'm afraid you'll have to start over. I'm so sorry."

I told her it was okay then after several minutes of listening to music again I was greeted by the voice of a Mrs. Porter.

"I understand you wish to register for Medicare," she said.

I began answering her questions, then at *city of birth* I replied, "Winthrop, Massachusetts"

"Oh," she said, "I live there."

"You live in Winthrop, Massachusetts and commute to Albuquerque, New Mexico?" I said.

"No, don't be silly. My office is in Boston. The O'Neill Building," she replied.

"I'm sitting in that lobby right now," I said.

"Then why don't you come up to my desk," she asked.

"I don't have an appointment."

"Don't be silly," she told me, "just come up."

. . .

The last time I had been in a SSA office was when my daughter Kouri was three and she had just been naturalized an American citizen. She didn't have a job yet but we thought we'd better get her a Social Security number anyway. Kouri and I walked into the office (then located at Government Center) and were directed to a clerk. We approached his desk.

"What a pretty little girl," he said, "What can I do for you?"

"She would like a social security number," I said.

"Oh that's easy. We have plenty of those. Her birth certificate, please."

I handed him her just issued, amended birth certificate. When Kouri arrived from Korea, she was accompanied by official travel papers but her birth certificate was sealed. Once she became a citizen here, we got an amended birth certificate showing her birthplace as Seoul, Donna as her mother, me as her father and

Cataldo as her family name.

"It all seems in order," he said then looked up at me and asked, "So when were you in Korea?"

"Oh, I've never been there," I answered.

"When was your wife last there?"

"Never. She's never been there either," I replied.

It was clear from his expression that he was trying to figure out how our daughter was born in a place that neither of us had ever been.

I let him think for a moment then helped; "She's adopted," I said.

"Oh, of course."

"Now, could we get on with..."

Kouri's social security number arrived by post a few days later.

...

Two months before my seventieth birthday, I received a letter; this time telling me that I *had to* start collecting social security benefits. Donna was getting a nice pension from her thirty years as a teacher, I was still working and we had money saved, so we were fortunate enough to not really need Social Security benefits. I called and got connected to a Mrs. Dennis and told her I would like to not collect the benefit right now but if things changed and I needed it, I'd let her know.

"Oh no," she said quite emphatically, "You *must* take the money."

"I must? ... What if I refuse?" I said.

"You can't," she informed me.

"I can't? Why not?"

"Because if you do, you'll be fined."

"Fined? How much is the fine," I asked.

"It's equal to the amount of your check."

I pondered this information for a moment then said, "Well, isn't that the same as me not taking the money?"

Aha! I thought, *I've got them!*

It was like a chess game and I was skillfully countering their every move.

"No," she said, "because you will have to pay the tax on it whether you take it or not!"

I paused, then offered, "That doesn't make any sense."

"It doesn't have to make any sense," she said, " ...that is how we do it." (Then I'm pretty sure I heard her say. *"Checkmate!")*

"Okay," I said, now resigned to my fate, "you win; send me the money."

The Social Security Administration sends out 78 billion dollars a *month*. Twenty-two transfers per second; every second... of every minute... of every day of the year.

Mine arrives on the fifth of the month.

Good Byes

I miss my Mom and Dad. The Mom and Dad that I remember from when I was eight, that is. They were always there for me but I was so busy growing up that I hardly noticed them. They were like furniture. Mom and Dad became people to me when old and frail and I had to help care for them.

My mother had Alzheimers, so I lost her years before she died and I regret I never got to say good-bye. Mom was everything to me when she was my Mom. She always sided with me in a dispute with my dad, always praised my efforts and laughed at my jokes well before the punchline. If she found out I liked a certain snack food, she would get it for me until I had so many, I had to give them away.

Unfortunately my father kept her body functioning for a long time after what made her my Mom, had gone. I guess he just couldn't let her go.

Dad, on the other hand, never stopped being Dad. He was a pain in the ass until the end. It was just part of his DNA, I guess.

After Mom died, his memory began to fail. He would pull his car out of the driveway onto the street then forget where he wanted to go. So my sister took his car away from him. He got angry and the following day, walked to a dealership in the next town but fortunately, by the time he got there, he forgot why he had gone.

"Your father is here and I have a feeling I shouldn't try to sell him a car," the salesman said on the phone.

"Right," I said, "I'll be there in thirty minutes."

Neighbors reported seeing him climb onto the roof of the three story building he lived in. I had to help him down the ladder that he had set up by himself.

When he reached ninety, our conversations were mostly concerned with events from the distant past, all of which he seemed able to recall clearly. I heard stories of his childhood exploits, many involving my now deceased aunts and uncles. He re-told stories often, which was okay, since it gave us something to talk about.

Sometimes while I was visiting he would forgot I was there. "When did *you* get here?" he would ask near the end of my hour-long stay.

Then one afternoon over coffee he said, "Do you know the smartest thing I ever did?"

I was startled to think that all those hours of visiting, drinking coffee and re-hearing the same stories over and over, were finally going to pay a huge dividend. This could be the knowledge I had always been waiting for.

"No. Tell me," I said, "What was the smartest thing you ever did?"

"I never had any children," he proudly announced.

A bit stunned, I recovered enough to gesture with my hands as I raised my eyebrows.

He studied me for a moment then inquired, "What? *You're* not my child, are you?"

"Yes... your youngest," I pointed out.

"I have more than one?" he said.

"Two," I said, "You have two."

At ninety-five, his physical health deteriorated rapidly as well. He was soon in the hospital, where my sister and I had, in accord with his wishes, decided that he should be kept comfortable but no extraordinary measures taken. I visited him on a late fall evening to find that he had punched a young female doctor and given her a black eye. She was not the first doctor he had punched so they had restrained his arms in the bed.

"Can I remove the restraints while I'm with him," I asked the head nurse.

"Yes, if you promise to call us to put them back on when you leave. I'm sure Dr. Sanpour would appreciate it."

"I'm so sorry that happened," I said, "I'll be sure to call you when I'm going to leave."

I removed the straps from his arms. He could barely speak due to a stoke but he made an effort to smile a "thank you." I sat with him, holding his hand for maybe a half hour telling him about my day and the grand-kids and the like. Then I looked at my watch.

"Well, I'm going to go now Dad. I'll come by tomorrow," I said.

Dad watched as I pushed the call button for the nurse.

He got agitated and shook his head, *"No."*

"Dad, I have to. You can't be punching doctors," I maintained.

He grabbed my arm and pulled me closer. He was still remarkably strong (which made me feel even worse for Doctor Sanpour.)

When he got my head even with his, he strained to speak one word as distinctly as he could.

"Bastard," he said.

The nurse came in to put the restraints back on. I couldn't watch, so I walked out to my car.

He passed away later that night.

I don't know the first word he ever uttered to me, but I won't ever forget the last one. I like to think he meant it in a good way.

. . .

The wake was held a few days later and it was thought that perhaps it might not be appropriate for the grandchildren (especially six year old Jaramie) to see Grampy lying in the casket. When they arrived the following day for the funeral, Jaramie walked around and spotted the closed casket waiting to be loaded into the hearse for its trip to the cemetery.

"Where's Grampy," she inquired.

"He's there in that casket," I answered.

"Are you sure," she asked, "How do you know?"

I thought for a second then replied, "Well, he was in there last night but... that's a good question; I'll check."

I went and stopped the funeral director as he scurried around attending to the many details; lining up cars, arranging flowers, etc.

"Excuse me," I said, "My granddaughter doesn't think her Grandpa is in that box."

Now, I know that a sense of humor is something a good funeral director must suppress but this fellow had evidently extinguished his completely.

He stopped moving, the blood appeared to drain from his face and he defensively replied, "Of course he is!"

"Well, she's not so sure. How can we convince her?"

He didn't move a muscle.

"Now *I'm* not so sure," I said, "maybe we should show her the body," I said half in jest.

"But it's locked. I'd have to get the key," he said.

Jaramie and I held our ground and stood silently.

"Alright, wait in the next room," he ordered.

A few minutes later the director reappeared and allowed us in. We entered the room to see the casket standing open with a red velvet kneeling bench along side. Jaramie approached and stood on the bench.

"Why is he so white," she asked.

"Because he's dead," I answered somewhat indelicately, "That's what you look like."

She contemplated the body for a moment then lifted her arm, straightened out a finger and poked Grampy's side as hard as she could. The funeral director gasped. Jaramie turned to face us.

"Okay, he's dead!" she confirmed.

Walking to our assigned automobiles for the ride to the cemetery we asked Jaramie if she would like to ride in the big black limousine with us. Excitedly she accepted the offer and stood up for the whole trip explaining how this was her very first ride in a limousine.

As the procession turned into the burial ground, she looked at us, beamed and said, "This is the *best* day of my *whole* life!"

My dad would have truly loved that moment. It was a perfect goodbye at the end of a good life.

Remembering Pete and me

I have never won a game of chance except this once at a carnival in Winthrop, when I was eight years old, and I threw a dart and broke the red balloon and won a parakeet. His name was Pete. Well actually, I don't know what his name was, and no matter how hard I tried I couldn't get him to talk, so I called him Pete. But he was great fun and flew around the kitchen and landed on my shoulder and bit my ear and made my Aunt Tina scream because she thought he would get tangled in her hair. Pete pooped everywhere, spilled those little seed coverings all over and landed in the sugar bowl once in a while, but still I thought he was great.

Then one day he got sick. I begged my Mom to call a vet and she finally did only to be told that Pete had an incurable brain infection common to parakeets. It wasn't long before I found him on the bottom of the cage and had to begin planning his memorial service. I put him and some crumpled newspaper in a shoe-box, borrowed from Mom's closet, wrapped it in Saran Wrap and carried it out to the yard. I had to unwrap him twice to prove to my cousins that there was indeed a dead parakeet in the box, but I finally got him in his shallow hand-dug grave behind one of dad's rose bushes. I pushed a stick into the ground to mark the spot and we stood silently for a few seconds.

"Shouldn't we say something," cousin Dotty whispered.

I thought for a moment then said, "Good-bye Pete."

I kept thinking of Pete, underground, being eaten by bugs and I ended up sleeping with the light on that night. Maybe that's why I would just as soon be cremated. (I suppose I could have cremated Pete, except I wasn't allowed to play with matches.)

Many years later, I was renovating offices in a building in the Mount Auburn Cemetery. The crematorium was in the basement and I could feel the heat from the oven all the way across the hall whenever I passed by.

It seemed to always be hot down there, so one day I asked one of the employees, "How long does it take the oven to cool down?"

"Don't know," he replied, "Why?"

"So you can clean it out between the bodies," I said.
"Clean it out?" he answered. He seemed puzzled.
"I mean, after one body... but before the next."
"Oh," he said, "follow me," and motioned me into an adjacent room.
"See that chart on the wall?" he asked rhetorically.
The chart had a *male* and *female* column and weight *before* and weight *after* rows.
"Mrs. Smith goes in... and she weighs a hundred pounds... " he pointed to the chart, "...we take out four pounds, 2 ounces of ashes like it says. Then Mr. Jones goes in... he's one hundred eighty pounds... and... the chart says six pounds, eleven ounces come out. That chart says it all. You get the picture now, don't ya?"
I made a surprised face.
"I can't remember the last time we cleaned that thing. Don't matter; we all the same color ashes, you know," he chuckled.
He was right of course. One carbon atom is indistinguishable from any other. That's another reason that cremation makes sense to me, I suppose.
But even if there's no body in a casket, everyone should have a memorial service of some kind and I think it would be cool if I could be at my own. I'd see the little container of ashes (six pounds, 8 ounces maybe) sitting in the middle of a table with a hastily framed picture of me next to it to help with the illusion that I'm in the room. Donna (already planning her extended stay in Venice) and a few friends are there along with my children and grand-children; and who knows, maybe a great grand-kid or two as well.
There's plenty to eat-- my favorite foods perhaps-- your choice of peanut butter and jelly sandwiches or tuna melts if it's lunchtime or grilled swordfish in the evening, washed down with a really cold beer or seltzer water. And of course, bread or rice pudding (with no raisins) for dessert.
I wouldn't be surprised if someone says, *"They don't make 'em like him anymore,"* or *"He'll sure be missed,"* but that will be about it. No need to dwell on death when there are still things to be done.
But here's what I've figured out; physical things, like buildings and statues and your body, come and go, crumble, fall down and

disappear, but if you make memories you'll stay around for a long while. Heck-- I still remember Pete. He made it into this story and all he did was bite my ear once or twice sixty-five years ago. Is Pete really gone? I say no. I remember Pete because in his little way he made a memory for me and that helped make me who I am.

So I guess I shouldn't have said "*good-bye*" to Pete, I should have said "*thank you.*"

The way I see it, if I'm lucky, after the memorial that little container of ashes will remain on the table, but I'll be leaving with the kids.

Afterward

When I began writing this book I had no idea how much fun I would have. It seems there is no end to the number of wonderful and interesting people who helped me become who I am and it was a pleasure to rediscover and be with them again for a while.

There were many more stories I wanted to tell but my desire to tell them was not matched by my ability as a writer.

In any case, I hope you enjoyed reading these stories as much as I enjoyed writing them.

And even if, as it turns out, I'm not so perfect, you have to admit it's a catchy title.

Acknowledgment

First, I want to thank all the family members and friends who urged me to write these stories down.

Thanks to my daughter-in-law, Jennifer who helped edit the book and get my commas under control.

I had the good fortune to take two writing classes at Harvard Extension School from Myra McLarey who gave me the insights and confidence that stayed with me and, after many years, helped me to finally write this book.

I guess I have to thank Miss McIntyre (my twelfth grade writing teacher) who, despite the fact that we didn't see eye-to-eye on most things, taught me how to write a reasonable sentence.

Thanks to my Mom for always standing up for me and Dad for making me believe that I could do anything.

And special thanks to my wife, Donna who not only helped me recollect the memories but helped me make them.

Made in the USA
Middletown, DE
03 June 2018